THE CATHOLIC WARRIOR

Robert Abel

VALENTINE

Valentine Publishing House
Denver, Colorado

Cover Graphics – Desert Isle Design LLC

Publisher's Cataloging-in-Publication Data
    Abel, Robert.
    The Catholic Warrior / Robert Abel — 3rd ed.

    p. cm.
    Includes bibliographical references.
    Preassigned LCCN : 2003-108071
    ISBN-10 : 0-9711536-0-4
    ISBN-13 : 978-0-9711536-0-8

    1. Bible – Quotations.
    2. Christian life – Catholic authors.
    3. Catechetics – Catholic Church.
    4. Christianity.
    5. Spiritual warfare.
    6. Faith – Biblical teaching.
    7. Angels.
    8. Demonology. I. Title.

    BX2350.3 .A24 2004
    248.4' 82–dc21
    2003-108071

Printed in the United States of America.

The *Catholic Warrior* is a brilliant treatise on spiritual warfare that boldly confronts the ferocity of the enemy and his evil minions by forthrightly exposing their devious stratagems. Robert Abel has taken up the gauntlet of holy audacity in persuasively urging his readers to engage as heroic warriors in the ongoing battle against the evil one. He shows that in this great endeavor, it is truly a privilege as well as an obligation to don the armor of battle and align oneself inextricably with the power of Jesus in facing life's most formidable challenge — advancing the kingdom of heaven here on earth.

FATHER JOHN H. HAMPSCH C.M.F.

TABLE OF CONTENTS

Proclaim this among the nations:
Prepare war, stir up the warriors. Let all
the soldiers draw near, let them come up.

Beat your plowshares into swords,
and your pruning hooks into spears;
let the weakling say, "I am a warrior."

Joel 3:9–10

1

CHAPTER ONE

THE VISION

VATICAN CITY, ROME — In a state of astonishment, I passed through several rows of towering stone columns. They rose magnificently from the ground with all their strength reaching toward heaven. Hundreds of them, all in perfect alignment, supported two semi-circular colonnades, one on each side of the Basilica.

Even the cobblestones beneath my feet were singing praises to God. I knelt down to touch one that looked a thousand years old. As I rubbed my fingers over the smooth black surface, my spirit started praising God. I felt as though I were in a different world, disconnected from the crowds of tourists flurrying around me.

For a brief moment the crowd parted and I caught a glimpse of a magnificent obelisk in the center of Saint Peter's Square. The slender structure directed my attention toward the heavens. As I looked up, I caught sight of a vast army. On top of the colonnade stood hundreds of holy men and women of God. They were looking down at me as if from the upper levels of a stadium.

All at once they started cheering with one accord. I

felt as though I were surrounded by the *great cloud of witnesses* from Hebrews 12. They were cheering for me to enter the race. I could hear the words stirring in my heart, "Run in such a way as to win the prize!"

Looking around to see who was there, I noticed John the Baptist, Saint Andrew, and Thomas Aquinas. With swords and staff in hand, they were ready for action. Some carried crosses; others were reading from scrolls and displaying banners of victory. Standing at the center, holding a cross in his hand, was the Commander of the Lord's army himself — Jesus!

It was like a view of heaven. All the renowned warriors of old were interceding for the saints on earth. Once these holy men and women enter the heavenly realm, they continue to intercede for lost souls on earth.

As the battle cries and shouts for victory continued, the valiant role models were inspiring me with their words of encouragement: "Put on the full armor of God so that you will be able to stand firm against the wiles of the devil." Their words inspired a burning strength deep within my heart. In that moment, I could have accomplished anything!

Reality check — I'm a Catholic tourist in a foreign country. There's a priest shortage in America and I attend a parish with 3,000 families run by one man. My pastor is so busy he probably works fifteen hours a day. After all the weddings, funerals, baptisms, and late-night emergency calls, it's a wonder he has time to prepare a homily on Sunday.

The valiant warriors surrounding me had *conquered*

kingdoms, administered justice, obtained promises, shut the mouths of lions, quenched raging fire, escaped the edge of the sword, won strength out of weakness, became mighty in war, and put foreign armies to flight.[2]

Saint Paul was beaten with rods three times, stoned to the point of death, shipwrecked for a night and a day, *in toil and hardship, through many a sleepless night, hungry and thirsty, often without food, cold and naked.*[3] And besides other things, he was constantly under the daily pressure and anxiety from the newly established Church.

Today, the average parishioner only attends Mass on Sunday, yet every spirit-filled Christian has been given the power to accomplish the same works as Jesus according to John 14:12, which says, *"Very truly, I tell you, the one who believes in me will also do the works that I do and in fact, will do greater works than these..."*

Can you imagine a vast army of spiritual warriors doing greater works than Jesus? The Bible not only says it's possible, Mark 16:17–18 says it's a fact that should accompany all believers. *These signs will accompany those who believe: by using my name they will cast out demons; they will speak in new tongues; they will pick up snakes in their hands, and if they drink any deadly thing, it will not hurt them; they will lay their hands on the sick, and they will recover.*

You have already been given the power. Jesus gave his disciples the *authority to tread on snakes and scorpions, and over all the power of the enemy.*[4] All you need is a belief in Jesus — just enough faith to start doing the same works he did, and soon you will be doing even greater works. That's because Jesus went to the Father to send us the Spirit. Jesus promises to do whatever we ask in his name so that his Father will be glorified.

All you need is faith the size of a mustard seed and you will say to the mountain, *Move from here to there, and it will move; and nothing will be impossible for you.*[5] Faith is more than an intellectual belief or an embodiment of religious doctrine. Faith is the instrument a warrior uses to bring down the power of God into every situation that seems impossible.

There's a great cloud of witnesses cheering every warrior toward the battle line. All you need to do is put on the full armor of God and start fighting the good fight of faith. As a disciple of Christ you have already been given the power.

God is looking for anyone who is willing to stand in the gap and advance the kingdom of heaven here on earth. The battle is fierce, the rewards immense, and the adventure beyond your wildest dreams. *The Spirit and the bride say, "Come."*[6] Come join the holy army of God.

The whole of man's history has been the story

of dour combat with the powers of evil,

stretching, so our Lord tells us, from

the very dawn of history until the last day.

This dramatic situation of the whole world,

which is in the power of the evil one,

makes man's life a battle.

Catechism of the Catholic Church: 409

1

CHAPTER TWO

THE ENEMY

Many years ago I met a lady named Athena who could see into the spiritual realm. As our friendship developed, she started to detect an unhealthy presence in me that arose in social settings. Whenever I went to a night club or a crowded social environment where beautiful women were present, my personality would change. My everyday self would disappear, and a "player" personality would take over.

The behavior wasn't driven by lustful or sexual thoughts; it was driven more from the sin of coveting. I would long for a beautiful woman by my side, but as soon as she gave me her heart, I wanted someone prettier. I was never satisfied. I could be on a date with Miss California and would still be checking out the room for another tall, beautiful blonde.

My player personality could show up anytime, except it didn't have the same force without a supernaturally charged environment. It liked feeding on the crowded, dark, dance clubs where people were "hitting" on each other.

I had tried to eliminate this behavior a year before meeting Athena. I talked to many friends about it, but no one could offer any insight. If they confronted me about going to the bars in the first place, I would defend my behavior with statements such as, "Jesus was social."

Athena could see the problem from a mile away. She tried talking to me about demonic oppression, but I didn't want to hear it. Then one day while I was talking to her on the phone, the topic came up again. This time I said, "I'm into self-work. Bring it on! I hereby put myself on the Lord's operating table."

Instantly, a demonic presence appeared right in front of me. I could see it with my spiritual eyes. It looked like a purple, transparent piece of film that was covering my entire body. When the Spirit of the Lord struck it, the demon folded in half. As soon as the top half of my body was free from it, I could see and feel its presence in the lower half.

It was the most horrible, filthy presence I had ever encountered. It was like a black hole of pure hate that was invading my space. My first reaction was that of great violation. It was trespassing. An unwanted intruder not only appeared in my house, but it had attached itself to my person like a filthy leech.

"What's happening?" Athena kept screaming on the phone.

"I don't know, but it was the sickest, most disgusting... I don't know what you were praying, but I gotta go."

"No wait! We have to pray some more."

She was able to calm me down and introduce me to spiritual warfare. After getting off the phone with her, I started researching Sacred Scripture. I found over a hundred listings in my Bible's concordance for the word demon. It turns out, spiritual warfare was a major part of Jesus' ministry; he came to preach the Good News, cure the sick, and cast out demons.

The first verse I came across said that Satan was the *ruler of this world.*[2] Jesus made the same point standing in front of Pilate: *"My kingdom is not from this world. If my kingdom were from this world, my followers would be fighting to keep me from being handed over to the Jews. But as it is, my kingdom is not from here."*[3]

When Jesus was fasting in the wilderness, Satan led him up and showed him in an instant all the kingdoms of the world. Afterwards Satan said to Jesus, *"To you I will give their glory and all this authority; for it has been given over to me, and I give it to anyone I please. If you, then, will worship me, it will all be yours."*[4] Of course, Jesus refused, but Satan couldn't offer Jesus all the kingdoms of the world if they didn't belong to him in the first place.

Not only is Satan the ruler of this world, but *he was a murderer from the beginning and does not stand in the truth, because there is no truth in him. When he lies, he speaks according to his own nature, for he is a liar and the father of lies.*[5] At first I didn't want to believe it, but after my eyes had been opened, I had no choice. I heard gospel stories about demons, but I didn't know what to believe until I met evil face to face.

The very next day the "Bud Girls" called and asked me to go out. Stephanie and Victoria never called me. I always had to call them, plus pay their cover charges and buy drinks all night. As soon as Stephanie offered the invitation, a war began in my soul. A part of me wanted to cruise the bars, to be social and dance, but another part was scared to death. I knew the invitation was a trap set by evil to snare my soul. But this time, instead of one purple demon, I might end up with seven more. I couldn't stop thinking about a verse from Luke:

> *When the unclean spirit has gone out of a person, it wanders through waterless regions looking for a resting place, but not finding any, it says, "I will return to my house from which I came." When it comes, it finds it swept and put in order. Then it goes and brings seven other spirits more evil than itself, and they enter and live there; and the last state of that person is worse than the first.*[6]

It was extremely difficult but I finally told Stephanie, "No! I'm sorry but I can't go out tonight." Of course, she wanted to know why, but I didn't have the courage to tell her the real reason. I made up an excuse. After getting off the phone with her I called Athena and said, "I'm worried more demons will come back. Is there some kind of prayer you can say to make them go away?"

"You can't make demons go away! The bars are full of demons and they have every right to be there."

"Then how do I protect myself?"

"You have to keep yourself pure and holy. Then figure out how the demon gained access to your inner sanctuary in the first place. Once you identify the open door, ask Christ to seal it shut."

"How do I do that? I don't even know what door you're talking about."

"It may take a lot of prayer. The doors are usually hidden and often heavily guarded. A lot of times, demons will use repressed emotional baggage like traumatic experiences from your past. Just keep praying; I'm sure Christ will show you the way."

After getting off the phone with Athena, I started the process by giving the demon a name. I called it the demon of Female-Carnal-Desire because now my sin of coveting felt more like a carnal desire. As I searched for open doors, the only thing I could identify was my social list. I had over a hundred names and phone numbers of single women. They were mostly friends, distant acquaintances, girls I had gone out with once or twice.

After searching my heart, I realized the need to break all bonds with my old game-playing behaviors. I imagined being married and how my future wife would feel about my social list. Surely she wouldn't approve, but for some reason, I couldn't let it go. It felt as though a part of my soul was attached to the list — like it was a trophy case I used to feed my ego. Having the girls' numbers made me feel popular, like a stud. Only after a lot of prayer was I able to set it on fire and release it to the Lord.

After breaking all unhealthy bonds and soul-ties, and removing the source of my temptation, I still needed to discover the open door. It took me several weeks of prayer in front of the Blessed Sacrament, but eventually the Lord brought back the memory. When I was thirteen years old, I found a *Playboy* magazine in a dumpster behind the shopping mall. I hid it under my mattress for about a month. Every so often, I would look at the pictures and read a column called *Forum*. At the time, I thought it was the best text ever because as I read it, a burning heat would sweep over me.

One day while reading a sexually perverted story, the erotic, burning heat came over me. I liked it so much that I wanted more. I wanted to take the heat, the feelings, the erotic passion inside of me. Without knowing what I was doing, I made an agreement in the spiritual realm and the demon of Female-Carnal-Desire entered my being.

Over the years the demon did everything it could to pervert me sexually and interfere in my relationships with women. I fought it through the power of my free will and by going to daily Mass. I made a vow of sexual celibacy until marriage. Whenever a lustful thought entered my mind, I quickly dismissed it; yet the demon continued to hold on because of the unconfessed sin on my soul.

Even though I attended Confession regularly, the demon had a right to access my soul because I never made a true act of contrition. At the time, I may have even confessed the sin of lust, but it wasn't a true confession, because I was never truly sorry. A part of me liked the burning heat and the lustful sensation that swept over me.

After the Lord showed me the breach in my inner sanctuary, I begged his forgiveness. I hadn't looked at pornography since the time I was thirteen years old, but after I discovered the open door, I immediately went to Confession and sealed it shut.

Afterwards I felt stronger than ever. I had replaced

the void in my soul that the demon occupied with the Holy Spirit. My player personality was completely nonexistent. I couldn't even go into the bars anymore. They made me sick. The game-playing womanizer was completely gone.

After conducting more research, I found out the Catholic Church performs two kinds of exorcisms. The first one is called a simple exorcism and is performed when someone is baptized. After anointing the catechumens with oil, the celebrant lays hands on them and says a short prayer.

The other type of exorcism the Catholic Church performs is when someone is totally possessed. It's called a major exorcism and can be performed only by a special priest who first needs permission from a Bishop.

In a case of demonic possession, the victim is consumed with an evil presence, like in the movie *The Exorcist*. Demons have taken control of the victim's body and are able to speak and act without the victim's consent. Many times the victims scream profanities, possess super-human strength, and need to be held down by friends and family members.

The Church covers two extremes: They say prayers over the elect at baptism and they have a team of specialists who can deliver those who are totally possessed. But what about the middle ground? In my case, I had already received the prayers at baptism, and I wasn't possessed. I picked up a demon reading an article in *Playboy*.

Saint Paul also had unpleasant experiences with demons. Three times he begged the Lord to deliver him. Paul wasn't possessed. He had been given a thorn in the flesh, a *messenger of Satan to torment* him.[7] Other holy men, like Saint Paul of the Cross and Saint Nicholas of Tolentino, have also had to fight demons as have godly women like Catherine of Siena and Saint Theresa of Avila.

Not only does Satan attack godly men, but he is every Christian's adversary. 1 Peter 5:8 says Satan prowls around like a roaring lion looking for someone to devour. Every day millions of Christians are assaulted by the presence of darkness. Like a deadly pestilence, demons have the ability to cause everything from minor medical problems to very serious illnesses like cancer, epilepsy, influenza, and leukemia. God didn't create disease; it all originated from Satan with the fall of Adam and Eve.

The Gospel writer Luke specifically points out two types of healings that Jesus performed. One type of healing was of medical conditions and the other type involved demons. For example, when Peter's mother-in-law was ill, Jesus *stood over her and rebuked the fever, and it left her. Immediately she got up and began to serve them.*[8]

In other cases, the patient may appear to be suffering from a medical condition, but after Jesus commands a demon to flee, the patient recovers. A good example is the young boy who was diagnosed with epilepsy, a chronic nervous disorder of the brain affecting consciousness and muscular control. Everyone was convinced the boy was untreatable. Yet Jesus *rebuked the demon, and it came out of him, and the boy was cured instantly.*[9]

The same thing happened with a woman who had been crippled for eighteen years. It was a medical problem being caused by demons. She was bent over and couldn't stand up straight. Demons entered the woman's body and attached themselves to her bones and muscles. They were interfering with the electrical impulses in her nervous system.

After diagnosing the problem, Jesus laid hands on her and said, *"Woman, you are set free from your ailment."*[10]

When the leaders of the synagogue became indignant because he healed on the Sabbath, Jesus showed them a more in-depth view of her situation. He responded, *"Ought not this woman, a daughter of Abraham whom Satan bound for eighteen long years, be set free from this bondage on the sabbath day?"*[11]

It wasn't a medical problem, it was bondage to Satan. Somewhere in her past she made an agreement with evil through her sinfulness and a demon developed a stronghold in her life. It may have started out with a simple temptation which gave way to a reoccurring sin, or it may have passed on from her parent's sins, in the form of emotional wounds.

After studying Scripture, I found out that demons have a need to dwell inside living creatures. They can experience emotions, express their desires, and speak through humans. They have the ability to make intelligent decisions and to network with other evil spirits. They can pool their powers together, possess in great numbers, and even exert great physical strength. A good example of all these abilities comes from the man at Gerasen.

After Jesus stepped out of the boat, *a man out of the*

tombs with an unclean spirit met him. He lived among the tombs; and no one could restrain him any more, even with a chain; for he had often been restrained with shackles and chains, but the chains he wrenched apart, and the shackles he broke in pieces; and no one had the strength to subdue him.

Night and day among the tombs and on the mountains he was always howling and bruising himself with stones. When he saw Jesus from a distance, he ran and bowed down before him; and he shouted at the top of his voice, "What have you to do with me, Jesus, Son of the Most High God? I adjure you by God, do not torment me." For he had said to him, "Come out of the man, you unclean spirit!"

Then Jesus asked him, "What is your name?"

He replied, "My name is Legion; for we are many."[12]

Now there on the hillside a great herd of swine was feeding; and the unclean spirits begged him, "Send us into the swine; let us enter them." So he gave them permission. And the unclean spirits came out and entered the swine; and the herd, numbering about two thousand, rushed down the steep bank into the sea, and were drowned in the sea.[13]

The demons used their ability to speak when they addressed Jesus as *Son of the Most High God.* They expressed their desires when they begged Jesus to send them *into the swine.* They wanted to inhabit a living being, whether it was the man or the pigs. There was a legion of them all working together, who gave the man the strength to wrench apart chains and break shackles into pieces.

One of the most common assaults demons inflict upon humanity comes in the form of temptations. Demons have the ability to insert thoughts into our minds. In fact, that's one of Satan's titles — the great *tempter*.[14] Every day Christians are bombarded with the tiny whispering voice that speaks everything from lies to sinful desires.

Other times demons will insert depressing and discouraging thoughts in a voice that sounds similar to the person's own internal dialogue. "I'm stupid. I can't do anything right. Nobody likes me." If the man agrees with these thoughts, he will start feeling discouraged. Instead of overcoming the obstacles that are blocking his path, he will lose energy and motivation. When prolonged over time, this kind of negative thinking will affect his brain chemistry and eventually lead to depression. If the downward spiral continues, it may even lead to thoughts of suicide.

Look at what happened to Job. After Satan manipulated the Chaldeans' thought processes and filled their hearts with malicious intent, they formed three columns and made a raid on Job's camels. They killed his servants with the edge of the sword and afterwards a great wind, influenced by the evil forces in nature, came across the desert and struck the four corners of his eldest son's house, causing it to collapse on the young people inside.

Satan even attacked Job's flesh with sickness and disease. The accuser of our comrades went before God's throne and obtained permission. Afterwards God said to Satan, *"Very well, he is in your power; only spare his life."* So Satan went out from the presence of the Lord, and *inflicted loathsome sores on Job from the sole of his foot to the crown of his head.*[15]

Satan is the ruler of this world, the roaring lion who prowls around looking for someone to devour, the accuser of our comrades, and the father of all lies. The thief only has one purpose, and that is to kill, steal and destroy. Demons can cause physical health problems, accidents, and disease. They have the power to destroy lives, marriages, and relationships.

Why would a loving God allow the devil to exist? The answer may completely change the way you view the world.

Behind the disobedient choice of our first parents lurks a seductive voice, opposed to God, which makes them fall into death out of envy. Scripture and the Church's Tradition see in this being a fallen angel, called Satan or the devil.

Catechism of the Catholic Church: 391

CHAPTER THREE

WORLDVIEW

One day God created a tropical paradise, a vast garden of colorful flowers and crystal-clear streams. Taking a handful of dust from the ground, God fashioned in his own image the crowning jewels of all creation, a man and woman named Adam and Eve. After breathing life into their physical bodies, they became spiritual beings.

All the angels in heaven marveled at God's masterpieces, except for one archangel named Lucifer. He was extremely jealous. It was his job to stand in attendance at God's throne and provide the heavenly court with songs of worship. He was the master of the heavenly choir and highly respected among the other angels.

Satan hated Adam and Eve because he used to be the center of attention. Everybody had loved his music, but now God had a new favorite. God loved the humans so much that he wanted them to live forever. He planted the Tree of Life in the center of the garden and intended to give them positions in the heavenly court higher than the angels.

Satan couldn't stand the idea. After he devised a plan and rounded up a third of the angelic army, a great *war broke out in heaven. Michael and his angels fought against the dragon. The dragon and his angels fought back, but they were defeated, and there was no longer any place for them in heaven. The great dragon was thrown down, the ancient serpent, who is called the Devil and Satan, the deceiver of the whole world — he was thrown down to the earth, and his angels were thrown down with him.*[2]

Then a loud voice in heaven cried out, *"Rejoice then, you heavens and those who dwell in them! But woe to the earth and the sea, for the devil has come down to you with great wrath, because he knows that his time is short!"*[3]

Satan and one-third of the heavenly host were stripped of their power and cast into the outer abyss. Everything that made them beautiful was taken away. All that was left was spiritual darkness, an empty void, a force of hate, bitterness, and anger.

Meanwhile, God continued to shower Adam and Eve with love and attention. He loved them so much that every evening he walked with them in the cool of the twilight. As Satan watched from the abyss, it made him furious. "How dare he make a mockery of the entire spiritual realm by having amorous liaisons with the humans," he said to the other demons.

"Let's get even with God and harm his most valuable possessions," one of the generals said.

"How's that possible?" one of the principality rulers asked.

"We'll make the humans violate the same spiritual law that caused our exile from God's presence," Satan said. "That way God won't be able to carry on his mushy love affair."

Being 100 percent spirit, the fallen angels could enter any of the animals, but Satan chose to enter the snake because it was the craftiest of all the Lord's creatures. Slowly he slithered up behind Eve. Catching her off guard he said, *"Did God say, 'You shall not eat from any tree in the garden'?"*[4]

"We can eat from all the trees," Eve said. "It's only the tree in the center of the garden that is forbidden. We're not even supposed to touch it, lest we die."

"You will not die! God knows full well, *when you eat of it your eyes will be opened, and you will be like God, knowing good and evil,"* Satan said.[5]

Seeing that the tree was good for food, a delight to her eyes, and had the ability to make her wise, Eve took the fruit and gave some to her husband. After they ate it their eyes were opened. They allowed a spirit of darkness to enter their souls and could no longer commune with God the same way as before.

Satan caused Adam and Eve to violate the first spiritual law of the universe — light and darkness can not be mixed together. Nothing evil can enter the Lord's presence. God could no longer interact with his beloved children in the same way, because they were tainted by sin. Not only did Adam and Eve need to be cleansed from all impurities, but they also needed to learn right from wrong.

Like a loving parent, God had known his children

couldn't live in the garden forever. At some point his children would need to grow up. Adam and Eve had a great time playing with the animals for many years, but Adam could never play cowboys and Indians. Both sides were always nice to each other. Without the presence of evil, there were only good guys and more good guys.

God in his great wisdom knew Adam and Eve would need to leave their childhood playground and start learning the lessons of life. That's why he set the tree in the center of the garden — almost as if he wrapped a large box with brightly colored paper, tied a red bow on top, and put it in the center of his child's room with a note attached: Do not open until you are ready to start school.

Adam and Eve didn't need any more education. They were created with a powerful intellect, a full vocabulary, and insight into mathematics, sciences, and the arts. What they needed was spiritual training, the kind that can only be taught through firsthand experiences. School books wouldn't be able to teach them holiness; they needed live interaction with a formidable opponent.

When God cast Satan and his vast army out of heaven, he stripped away their angelic powers. He left behind just enough strength to make them a dangerous opponent, yet weakened them to the point of harmlessness if Adam and Eve walked in complete obedience with God.

Satan had different ambitions. He was still the most intellectually advanced of all God's creatures. He devised a plan to take control over the entire earth. He wanted a kingdom of his own to rule, and the vast army of demons who followed him desperately needed something warm to inhabit.

Heaven was filled with light, warmth and love, and now the fallen angels were freezing in the abyss. They were starving for spiritual power and the only way to get it was to fight among themselves. Governors were attacking generals, and the seraphim were trying to force the lower-ranking cherubim into submission.

The fallen angels tried to reestablish the same order that flowed so beautifully in the heavenly court, but they couldn't. There was only intense hatred, and it caused all kinds of mutiny. It was total chaos until Satan stood up and said, "Stop attacking one another! Go forth and inhabit the humans. Cover the entire world with darkness."

"What's your plan, Master?" one of the generals asked.

"Fill Cain's mind with self-righteousness. Remind him how hard he works all day. Make him to keep the best produce for himself," Satan said.

When Cain and Abel came forward to present their offerings, God tried to use the opportunity to teach Cain valuable lessons between acceptable and non-acceptable sacrifices. But even more importantly, God wanted Cain's love and devotion. He wanted to establish a mutual love affair with his beloved child.

God allowed Satan to influence Cain with thoughts of anger and jealousy so that Cain would have a choice to make. God wanted him to choose love and obedience. He tried to help Cain on many occasions by asking, *"Why are you angry, and why has your countenance fallen? If you do well, will you not be accepted? And if you do not do well, sin is lurking at the door; its desire is for you, but you must master it."*[6]

The force of darkness lurking at Cain's door was too strong. A spirit of rage overpowered him and he killed his brother Abel. After the demons learned how to influence and manipulate humans, a vast cloud of darkness covered the land. The demons drove the entire human race into all kinds of sinful acts.

God continued to work with any man who was willing to walk in obedience. Men like Enoch who *walked with God; then he was no more, because God took him.*[7] God was using the resistance of evil to raise holy children. He was interested in acquiring precious stones. Out of all the grains of sand on the seashore, God was collecting diamonds.

Satan wanted to acquire large masses of people so that he could rule over them for all eternity. His vast army of demons covered the entire land with darkness. Eventually it grew so bad that God *was sorry that he had made humankind on the earth, and it grieved him to his heart. So the Lord said, "I will blot out from the earth the human beings I have created – people together with animals and creeping things and birds of the air, for I am sorry that I have made them."*[8]

Like a skilled surgeon, God amputated the diseased limb to save the patient's life. God took the only righteous man left, and asked him to build an ark. Soon the *waters that were under the dome* were released, and within forty days the earth was flooded.[9]

After the flood, the earth's population grew again. Out of his great love, which could not be quenched by his disappointment with humanity, God devised a new plan. This time he wanted to establish a holy nation. He wanted a people so loyal and obedient that they would never abandon or forsake his great love. He began the process by establishing a covenant with a man named Abraham, and through his lineage, the twelve tribes of Israel were born.

God wanted the twelve tribes to be a holy nation, a royal priesthood, a people set apart. He wanted to shower them with many blessings, to give them a land of their own, a land flowing with milk and honey. Before God could bring his new family into the Promised Land, he had to teach them the difference between right and wrong.

God allowed his children to fall into slavery at the hands of the Egyptians. He wanted to show them the ugliness of sin and experience it firsthand. He wanted his children to be so sick of the damage and destruction of evil that they would follow him in steadfast obedience.

After allowing his children to suffer 430 years of cruel slave labor, God sent Moses to work mighty wonders. He turned the Nile into blood and filled the Egyptians' ovens and kneading bowls with frogs. He sent locusts to destroy their crops and a deadly pestilence to kill their livestock. He sent an angel to strike down all the firstborn to show that it was not by luck or accident that they were set free, but only by the hand of God.

After the Egyptians set the Israelites free, God fed them manna in the desert when they were hungry, and water from a rock when they were thirsty. He cried out to them day and night, I want to be your God and I want you to be my people. After promising a land overflowing with milk and honey, the Israelites were ready to sign on the dotted line. Moses *took the book of the covenant, and read it in the hearing of the people; and they said, "All that the Lord has spoken we will do, and will be obedient."*[10]

Meanwhile, Satan and his vast army of demons continued to attack and pervert everything that was sacred to God. When God gave the command, *You shall not make for yourself an idol, whether in the form of anything that is in heaven above, or that is on the earth beneath,* the demons enticed people to carve wooden images.[11] They even granted spiritual powers to the worshippers. After luring the people to venerate the images, the demons pooled their powers together and granted the worshippers special signs and favors.

Whenever God's children sinned, they were required to pay the price for that sin with their own lives. Because God is a god of love, and takes no pleasure in seeing the destruction of the wicked, he allowed the penalty for sin to be transferred from the sinner's life onto the life of a sheep or goat. Whenever a man sinned, he could offer a sheep to the Levitical priesthood in place of his own life. After the animal was sacrificed, the blood was sprinkled on the altar and the sin was forgiven.

After successfully establishing a royal priesthood and a holy nation, God wanted the Israelites to take the same spiritual laws and advance them across the face of the earth. They were given the command to take possession of the land, over every place where the soles of their feet would tread. After forty years of spiritual training in the desert, the Israelites were ready to enter the Promised Land.

Before they crossed the Jordan, the Lord explained the reason why they needed to drive out all the other inhabitants. *When you come into the land that the Lord your God is giving you, you must not learn to imitate the abhorrent practices of those nations. No one shall be found among you who makes a son or daughter pass through fire, or who practices divination, or is a soothsayer, or an augur, or a sorcerer, or one who casts spells, or who consults ghosts or spirits, or who seeks oracles from the dead. For whoever does these things is abhorrent to the Lord; it is because of such abhorrent practices that the Lord your God is driving them out before you.*[12]

God takes no pleasure in the destruction of the wicked, but the Canaanites, Amorites, Hittites, Perizzites, Hivites, and the Jebusites had grown so wicked that they needed to be driven out or destroyed. Out of love for his children and so that his presence could dwell among them in a cloud by day and a pillar of fire by night, God commanded the Israelites to eradicate all forms of evil that refused to flee or change their ways.

Satan knew that the only way he could defeat the Israelites was to infiltrate the royal priesthood. So one day he called all the head demons together and said, "Assign your best religious spirits to the priests and leaders of the people."

"Why should we help them practice religion?" one of the generals asked.

"If we pervert their spiritual worship, God's presence will no longer accompany their armies. He will no longer bless the work of their hands," Satan said.

"That's impossible!" a demon cried out. "The Israelites are extremely religious. They will never stop performing sin offerings."

"Don't stop them," Satan said. "Just prevent true spiritual worship. Remove their focus from God and consume them with the behaviors of religion, like tithing on mint and dill. Make the practice of cleansing cups and dishes more important than the cleansing of their minds and hearts.

"Send in spirits of pride whenever the Pharisees take the seat of honor in the synagogue. Entice them to widen their phylacteries and broaden their fringes. Make the people worship the priests instead of God. Do anything you can to make the external practice of religion more important than the internal worship of God."

Satan's plan worked. Soon a cloud of darkness formed over the Israelite nation. God continued to send prophets who cried out to the people in the city square, *Thus says the Lord: I remember the devotion of your youth, your love as a bride, how you followed me in the wilderness, in a land not sown.*

"What wrong did your ancestors find in me that they went far from me, and went after worthless things, and became worthless themselves? I brought you into a plentiful land to eat its fruits and its good things. But when you entered you defiled my land, and made my heritage an abomination.

"Be appalled, O heavens, at this, be shocked, be utterly

desolate, says the Lord, for my people have committed two evils: they have forsaken me, the fountain of living water, and dug out cisterns for themselves, cracked cisterns that can hold no water."[13]

Satan's army had such a powerful influence over the religious leaders that every time a prophet delivered a message that conflicted with their way of life, they accused him of blasphemies, and stoned him to death. Before long the whole world was under evil's influence.

Yet God in his loving kindness continued to pursue his children. He sent his only begotten Son to establish a new covenant. Jesus stripped himself of divinity and took on the form of a slave. He left his heavenly throne and entered the world of darkness by becoming a man.

Satan kept a close watch on Jesus as he grew up. He wanted to discover Jesus' plans so that he could interfere and prevent his kingdom from being stripped away. He kept looking for opportunities to strike. He got his chance when Jesus was fasting for forty days in the wilderness.

Satan approached Jesus and said, *"If you are the Son of God, command these stones to become loaves of bread."*[14]

"One does not live by bread alone, but by every word that comes from the mouth of God," Jesus said.[15]

Then Satan took him to the pinnacle of the temple and said, *"If you are the Son of God, throw yourself down; for it is written, 'He will command his angels concerning you' and 'On their hands they will bear you up, so that you will not dash your foot against a stone.'"*[16]

"Again it is written, 'Do not put the Lord your God to

the test,'" Jesus said.[17]

After Satan realized he had no power over the Lord, he fled from his presence and called another meeting. He stood up in the midst of all the high-ranking demons and said, "I don't know what God is up to, but I don't like it. If Jesus keeps working miracles, the whole world will believe in him. They already worship the ground he walks on. Soon they will crown him king over Israel."

"Let's stir up a revolt," one of the generals suggested. "I will continue to harden the Pharisee's hearts. They already feel threatened. It won't take much."

"I will manipulate a few false witnesses," said a spirit of greed.

"Perfect," Satan said. "Incite a riot and let's kill the physical body of God. Then we will see what becomes of his plans."

A few days before Passover, the Romans were planning to crucify several criminals. Because Pontius Pilot was in town for a few days, the demons stirred an angry mob into action. They took Jesus into custody and started mocking him. One of the guards filled with a spirit of rage twisted a crown of thorns together and drove it in his skull. Everybody started laughing and spitting on him. "Look, it's the king of the Jews."

Like a lamb led to slaughter, Jesus was silent to fulfill the ancient prophecy.

Several guards stripped Jesus of his clothes and tied his hands to a post above his head. Another guard took a whip made of leather cords. It had sharp pieces of bone and rocks attached to the ends of the leather straps. The guard inflicted the full force of the whip across Jesus' back, shoulders, and legs.

At first the sharp objects cut through his skin. Then every time the guard brought it back for another assault, more and more of his flesh was torn away. It shredded his muscles and exposed his bones. Jesus' eyes were filled with tears, yet he continued to look at the men with love in his heart.

Finally, the guards untied Jesus and allowed his weak and bloody body to slump against the post. They threw a robe across his shoulders and placed a stick in his hand for a scepter. They mocked him, saying, *"Hail, King of the Jews!" They spat on him, and took the reed and struck him on the head.*[18]

After mocking Jesus, the guards stripped off the robe and tied a heavy cross to his shoulders. They forced him to begin the painful journey bearing the weight of the cross. Every time Jesus fell, another sting of the whip cut into his flesh. Eventually, he reached Golgotha, the Place of the Skull, where they crucified him.

Suddenly darkness covered the whole earth. All the sins of mankind fell upon Jesus. The Father had to turn away. Jesus cried out with a loud voice, *"My God, my God, why have you forsaken me?"*[19] Jesus became the sacrificial lamb of God. He paid humanity's price for sin, the penalty of death, with his own blood.

Afterwards there was a major shift in the spiritual realm. The curtain in the temple was torn in two. The earth shook. Rocks split. Tombs were opened and many bodies of the saints who had fallen asleep were raised. Satan never expected it to happen, but Jesus established a pipeline, a spiritual bridge between heaven and earth. In that instance, a sparkling beam of dazzling light broke through the darkness.

Before the Crucifixion God wanted to dwell with his children, but the darkness of sin separated him from his creation. Instead of destroying Satan, the source and instigator of darkness, and thereby depriving his children of the resistance they needed to grow in holiness, God sent his Son to establish a spiritual pipeline from heaven to earth — a conduit which allows his children to invite the presence of God into the darkness through the power of Jesus' love.

Jesus enacted the second spiritual law of the universe. If sin separates men from God, then love unites men with God, because God is love. When Jesus suffered all the abuse that Satan could inflict upon him, and remained loving, he broke Satan's power.

Now God's children can use the spiritual pipeline Jesus established between heaven and earth to invite God's love into the darkness anytime they want. God's children have become the light of the world.

How do God's children use the light of Christ to protect themselves and advance the kingdom of heaven here on earth? In the same way the strong man keeps his spiritual house intact.

How can one enter a strong man's

house and plunder his property,

without first tying up the strong man?

Then indeed the house can be plundered.

Matthew 12:29

1

CHAPTER FOUR

OPEN DOORS

Once upon a time a strong man and his wife entered a corrupt land of darkness. There were pickpockets on every corner, robbers who carried guns and thieves who stole anything that wasn't securely fastened. The only way the strong man could protect his family from the crimes and violence that continued both day and night was to build a mighty fortress.

After looking for land to build on, the strong man came across beautiful acreage with a running stream. On one side of the property, there was a small pond and a vast meadow of trees, on the other side was the most corrupt part of the city. The man and his wife loved the property so much they bought it in spite of its location.

After acquiring the deed, the strong man built four stone towers, one on every corner of his property. He enclosed the perimeter with a stone wall and posted "No Trespassing" signs along the outside walls. After the protective barrier was complete, he dug out the foundation and started building a fortified structure with rocks and mortar.

Within a year the project was complete. His family was able to move into a beautiful castle. There were many different levels, shiny tile floors, a rock terrace with stone archways, and all the exterior entrances were secured with beautiful handcrafted oak doors.

When it was finished, the strong man dedicated the property to the Lord. It was a secure sanctuary, a place where he could raise his family in love, a place of security from the outside world of thieves and robbers. All the strong man had to do was maintain the perimeter with constant security checks, and he would be safe.

Eventually, the strong man and his wife wanted to help the community. Children were starving in the streets due to overcrowded and impoverished conditions. Violent crimes were being committed in broad daylight. Every night someone was assaulted in the town square. Corruption had taken over the town's officials and the local law enforcement agency.

"I know how we can help," the strong man said. "Let's buy the most impoverished part of the city. After we build a protective barrier around the perimeter, we can drive out all the wicked inhabitants and plant crops for the people to eat."

"I have a better idea," his wife said. "Let's throw a banquet and invite all our neighbors for a party. After they see our love and hospitality, I'm sure they will want to know where it comes from. Maybe then we can help our neighbors change their ways."

"If we buy land we can feed them for many years."

"What better way to feed people than to invite them over for dinner?" his wife said.

Eventually, the man and his wife decided to throw a grand ball. They opened the doors of their home and invited their neighbors over for dinner. Within a few hours the guests had devoured all the food and started wandering around the castle.

"Where's the washroom?" one guest asked.

"Upstairs to the left," the strong man said.

As soon as the man reached the top landing, he entered the strong man's bedroom and began looking through the dresser drawers. After finding a gold watch and a pearl necklace, he put them in his pocket.

Meanwhile, another guest crept into the cellar and started removing screws from the window latches. He wanted to come back later that evening with some of his friends and steal everything in the storage area.

"Where's my purse?" the strong man's wife cried out. "It was sitting on the counter a minute ago."

Immediately the strong man realized the protective barrier surrounding his sanctuary had been breached. He turned to the guests and shouted, "How dare you steal from me!"

"You invited us here," one of the guests said.

"I invited you over for dinner, not so that you could steal from me."

"We're thieves and robbers," one of the guests said. "It's our job to steal."

"I demand the return of all my property, and that everybody leave immediately."

"You can't kick us out! You gave us an invitation.

We have the right to be here," one of the thieves said.

"If you don't leave, I will call the sheriff and have you arrested."

Suddenly, a fight broke out between the strong man and the thief who was wearing his watch. Most of the guests ran away into the darkness, carrying the man's property. Others started moving his fine artwork out the front door.

After several hours the sheriff from a neighboring village arrived and arrested the thieves who were still wrestling with the strong man. After they were taken to jail, the strong man and his wife learned a valuable lesson: Don't open the doors to your spiritual house and allow evil inside, because it's extremely difficult to get it to leave.

In the same way, every warrior needs to set up protective barriers around his spiritual house. In the Old Covenant, God wanted to dwell with his children in a cloud by day and a pillar of fire by night. In the New Covenant, God still wants to dwell with his children, but now he wants to dwell inside of everyone's heart.

All Christians are called to become temples of the living God, tabernacles for the Holy Spirit. In the same way the Israelites had to purge evil from their environment, it is imperative that all warriors invite Christ into their hearts, seal all the doors shut, and keep their spiritual houses clean.

There are seven common doors evil uses to enter a warrior's house and extinguish the light of Christ. By identifying these doors, you will be better prepared to protect yourself and your family from thieves and robbers whose only mission in life is to steal, kill, and destroy.

Door 1: Sinfulness

All sin is an agreement with evil. When a man commits sin, he is saying no to God, and yes to the devil. *Everyone who commits sin is a slave to sin.*[2] Sin is the door evil uses to gain access to your spiritual house. Once a pattern of sin has been established, demons can use the door anytime they want because sin gives them the key.

All sin seems innocent and harmless at first. A couple may share a romantic kiss on the cheek to say goodbye after a first date. After watching a movie later that week, they may find themselves on the couch making out. Once they start heavy petting and removing clothes, the sexual door has already been opened.

If the young lovers are not careful, their desires may give way to the sin of fornication, sexual relations outside of a marriage covenant. When their sin has fully grown, it will give birth to death because those who practice *such things will not inherit the kingdom of God.*[3]

Once a sexual door of sin has been opened in a relationship, it is extremely difficult to close it short of a breakup. Even after a breakup many couples continue to get back together for sexual flings. They can't pull away. The soul-ties and bonds are too strong because the two have *become one flesh.*[4] God designed sex to bond married couples together for a lifetime and he doesn't want any of his children bonded together with the wrong partner.

Even the desire of a single man to have sex is an open door for evil. Jesus says the man *who looks at a woman with lust has already committed adultery with her in his heart.*[5] Once he has made an agreement with evil, the tiny whispering voice will plague him late at night. If he agrees with the temptations, it will lead into deeper forms of sexual bondage. The only way to stop the cycle of destruction is to kick evil out of his house and invite the presence of Christ back inside.

Door 2: Emotional Wounds

Emotional wounds are breaches in the walls of a warrior's inner sanctuary. Even repressed wounds, like never receiving a parent's love or approval, will cause cracks that demons can use to gain access into a man's emotional and spiritual well-being. Demons have the ability to access these wounds because the lack of forgiveness violates God's law.

2 Corinthians 2:11 and Ephesians 4:27 both identify the lack of forgiveness as one of Satan's devices. True forgiveness is more than holding back anger and repressing feelings. True forgiveness is a function of the heart. It occurs only when you fully embrace your pain and invite God's love into the hurtful situation. The forgiveness process becomes complete only when God's love is able to flow through the interior pain and into the external circumstances that caused the pain in the first place.

Without working through the pain, evil can enter the wound anytime it wants and wreak all kinds of havoc. For example, women who have experienced the deepest possible hurt, sexual abuse, may never be able to establish a healthy relationship with a man until they work their way through the forgiveness process. Evil may drive them to become sexually promiscuous or frigid. They will either hate men for hurting them or blame themselves, and allow men to continue the cycle of abuse.

When a man has been with an unfaithful partner, he may never again be able to love another woman. Without working his way through the forgiveness process, he will relive the same feelings of mistrust and betrayal every time his wife is fifteen minutes late. Evil can poke his festering wounds anytime it wants and cause all kinds of relationship problems. Without working through the forgiveness process, there's no way to prevent darkness from extinguishing the lights in his spiritual sanctuary.

Door 3: Addictions

Almost all addictions are driven by demons that have rights to enter a man's soul through the first doorway of unconfessed sin or the second doorway of emotional wounds. For example, a gambling addiction may start out as entertainment, but when combined with the sin of greed, a thrill-seeking activity can quickly turn into an obsession. After a man has lost his marriage, all the money in his children's bank account, and the family house, he may desperately want to quit, but the demonic presence at work in his life continues to drive him back in search of one more winning streak.

In this situation there are only three forces at work: the gambler's free will, God, and the presence of darkness. Because *God cannot be tempted by evil and he him-*

self tempts no one, we know the addiction isn't being driven by God.[6] If the man wants to quit and can't, the only other possibility is the demonic. Demons have attached themselves to the unconfessed sin of greed in the man's soul and are influencing his behavior.

The same dynamics apply to eating, sex, drug, and alcohol addictions. If you're an overeater who wants to quit and can't, there's usually a third force at work driving your compulsive behavior. Instead of filling their inner sanctuary with the presence of God, most overeaters try to fill the aching need deep within their souls with the comfort and nourishment of food.

The best way for overeaters to break free from the addiction is to drive out the demons, seal the doors shut, and invite the presence of Christ to dwell inside their hearts.

Door 4: Alternative Spirituality

One of the main tactics demons use to hide their true nature is to disguise themselves as angels of deceptive light. For example, when Satan approached Adam and Eve in the Garden, he didn't present the truth — "Hi, I'm a fallen angel. I'm here to hurt you. Please have some fruit."

Satan speaks according to his nature: He is a liar and the father of all lies. When he approached Eve, he disguised *himself as an angel of light* and appeared in the form of a seductive temptation.[7] Satan said, "If you eat the fruit, you will become like gods yourselves, acquiring the knowledge of good and evil."

As in any good trap, the bait he used on Eve

appeared good and beneficial. Satan's words even contained some elements of truth, but once the victim opens the door of the trap, the hidden reality quickly consumes its prey.

The process of alternative spirituality may start out with something as innocent as horoscopes. On the surface they appear fun and entertaining, but there's a subconscious reason behind every action a man takes. If you have a desire to read horoscopes, you're not just reading text; you're looking for insight into your daily life. Instead of turning to God through prayer and fasting for answers, you're turning to a nebulous spiritual force for direction and guidance. When a man cries out to spiritual forces other than God, demons have every right to answer his call.

Palm readings, tarot cards, and crystal balls work the same way. Fortune tellers have an authentic gift to see into the spiritual realm, but instead of filling themselves with the gifts of the Holy Spirit, they make agreements with demons who give them the ability to see into other people's lives.

When a man approaches a psychic for a reading, the demons that have been assigned to the man communicate with the demons that the psychic is using. The readings become dangerous when the psychic asks, "Would you like to receive favors or blessings from the spiritual realm?" If you say yes, you are giving demons permission to enter your soul.

There's great power in all the practices of the "new age" movement. When a man practices dream channeling, astral projection, or seeks oracles from the dead, an actual spiritual presence will assist his efforts. It will give him the power to project his consciousness, travel in the spiritual realm, and offer him insight into the future. If you engage in these practices, you will be interacting with the angel of light — a demon disguised in the form of something good, whose only intention is the destruction of your soul. The Catholic Church condemns all such practices:

All forms of divination are to be rejected: recourse to Satan or demons, conjuring up the dead or other practices falsely supposed to 'unveil' the future. Consulting horoscopes, astrology, palm reading, interpretation of omens and lots, the phenomena of clairvoyance, and recourse to mediums all conceal a desire for power over time, history, and, in the last analysis, other human beings, as well as a wish to conciliate hidden powers. They contradict the honor, respect, and loving fear that we owe to God alone.[8]

Door 5: Witchcraft

Most witches join an existing coven where they make blood pacts with the devil. They sell their souls to Satan in exchange for an assignment of demons to carry out their spells. Many occult members also sell their children's souls and dedicate their entire family lineage to Satan as well.

These practices operate under the same spiritual laws as infant baptism. If God allows parents to dedicate their children to the kingdom of light as infants, he also allows children to be dedicated to the kingdom of darkness. If an infant can receive the gift of the Holy Spirit at baptism, he can also receive the curse of demons when offered to Satan.

When a witch casts a spell, demons are dispatched to bring the spell into effect. Curses work the same way, except they are usually backed with malicious intent. After a coven forms a concrete image of the victim, the witches call upon their demonic powers and reinforce them by projecting their anger in the spiritual realm.

Door 6: Unhealthy Soul-Ties

A good example of a healthy soul-tie comes from 1 Samuel 18:1: *The soul of Jonathan was bound to the soul of David, and Jonathan loved him as his own soul.* It's similar to a marriage where a man and his wife are joined together and become one flesh. When the presence of evil attacks the man, his wife will also feel the repressions through the spiritual ties that have been established. God designed the intimate bonds of marriage this way to help the couple support one another during the hard times.

A harmful soul-tie is when a man's soul becomes attached to an unhealthy relationship. A good example of this is the sin of fornication. If you were to have sexual relations with anyone outside of a God-approved marriage covenant, a part of your soul will become attached to your partner's soul. It works like adjoining doors in a hotel room because the demons can use the tie to traffic back and forth between parties. That's why the sin of fornication is so harmful. *Every sin that a person commits is outside the body; but the fornicator sins against the body itself.*[9]

The Lord does not want his children *mismatched with unbelievers. For what partnership is there between righteousness and lawlessness? Or what fellowship is there between light and darkness? What agreement does Christ have with the Beliar? Or what does a believer share with an unbeliever? Therefore come out from them, and be separate from them, says the Lord, and touch nothing unclean.*[10]

It's also possible to develop unhealthy ties with situations and objects. Anything you set up on the altar of your heart can become a false god. Anything you use to feed your ego or boost your self-esteem, whether it be a Corvette, a social list, or basketball trophies, can become a false god and a doorway for evil to violate your inner sanctuary.

Door 7: Passivity

When a warrior fails to occupy his spiritual house, there are plenty of trespassers who will inhabit the property in his absence. Passivity is like going on vacation and leaving all the windows open. When a man lets his spirit wander, or fails to use his spirit to praise God in spirit and in truth, there are plenty of forces at work in the world who will help guide his attention.

There are many other doors that evil uses such as vows. When a man gets hurt and says the words, "I will never love another woman again," he is making a vow in the spiritual realm. Demons can enter his emotional wound and will try to hold the man to his own words.

Another door evil uses is deception. Satan is a liar. One false belief can throw your walk with God into a state of complacency. Lies can cause division in a church, destroy marriages, and annihilate friendships. Deception is the seductive and alluring ideas that evil

can use to trick you into opening your spiritual house
to strangers.

Lies are what caused the strong man and his wife to
invite thieves and robbers into their castle. After the
strong man identified the breach in his security system,
he had to fight the lies with the truth — and the truth
was able to set him free. After the strong man evicted
all the thieves and robbers from his castle, he closed all
the doors and sealed them under lock and key.

The very next day the strong man began buying
land. He went into the most corrupt part of the city,
and after acquiring a large parcel, he built four stone
towers, one in every corner. He enclosed the perimeter
with stone walls and posted "No Trespassing" signs
along the outside walls.

Once a protective barrier was established, he drove
out all the wicked inhabitants. He hired ethical workers
and planted crops for the town's people to eat. Before
long he had acquired all the land surrounding his beautiful castle for miles on every side. All the wicked inhabitants were either driven from his territory or forced to
conform to the strong man's standards of righteousness.

He took control over his kingdom through the
power of authority.

1

CHAPTER FIVE

TAKING AUTHORITY

God spent forty years helping the Israelites close all the doors that were open in their camp. In Exodus 32, he helped them close the door of idolatry when they fashioned a golden calf. In Numbers 14, he helped them close the door of rebellion when their spies brought back a negative report. In Numbers 25, he helped them close sexual doors when an Israelite man had intercourse with a Midianite woman in the sight of the whole congregation.

After fine-tuning their priesthood, incorporating all the laws of holiness, and establishing a pure inner sanctuary, the Israelites were ready to advance their territory. God wanted them to take the same principles of holiness and advance his kingdom through the entire land of Canaan.

After the death of Moses, God said to Joshua, *"Proceed to cross the Jordan, you and all this people, into the land that I am giving to them, to the Israelites. Every place that the sole of your foot will tread upon I have given to you, as I promised to Moses. Only be strong and very courageous, being careful to act in accordance with all the law that my servant Moses commanded you. Be strong and courageous; do not be frightened or dismayed, for the Lord your God is with you wherever you go."[2]*

God sent the Israelites to take possession of the land. Every place where the soles of their feet would tread, they were to drive out evil. The land belonged to the Lord, and when he passed the authority to his children, the Israelites became the official owners.

After 40,000 warriors crossed the Jordan and set foot in the Promised Land, Joshua saw a man standing before him with a drawn sword in his hand. Joshua approached him and said, *"Are you one of us, or one of our adversaries?"[3]*

"Neither," the man replied. "I am the *Commander of the army of the Lord."[4]*

At once Joshua fell on the ground and worshiped him. Afterwards he asked, *"What do you command your servant, my Lord?"[5]*

The Commander said, *"I have handed Jericho over to you, along with its king and soldiers. You shall march around the city, all the warriors circling the city once. Thus you shall do for six days, with seven priests bearing seven trumpets of rams' horns before the ark.*

On the seventh day you shall march around the city seven times, the priests blowing the trumpets. When they make a long blast with the ram's horn, as soon as you hear the sound of the trumpet, then all the people shall shout with a great shout; and the wall of the city will fall down flat, and all the people shall charge straight ahead."[6]

For six days the Israelites marched around the city.

Every man was silent. On the seventh day, God's warriors marched around the city, followed by the trumpeters, the Ark of the Covenant, and the rear guards. As soon as the people heard the sound of the trumpets they raised a great shout.

In the spiritual realm, there was another army standing by — God's angels. They were hovering over the walls of Jericho with flaming swords in hand. On the seventh march around the city, when all the people shouted, the angelic warriors touched the walls of Jericho with the tips of their flaming swords and instantly they crumbled. Afterwards the Israelites charged forward and won the battle.

Satan knew that to stop God's army of 40,000 men who were going to rid the land of evil, he would have to find another open door. He quickly dispatched demons and said, "Find a weak link. Apply pressure until one of them snaps."

"We've tried everything. They're invincible," one of the demons said.

"Who asked your opinion?" Satan said as he shoved the demon out of his way. "I don't care how you do it, turn up the heat and make them sin!"

Meanwhile the Israelites were preparing for their next battle against the kingdom of Ai, a small city near Beth-avan. When the Israelites attacked the city, the men of Ai overpowered them and killed thirty-six Israelite warriors.

After hearing the report, the hearts of the Israelites melted. All the elders put dust and ashes on their heads. Joshua tore his clothes and fell to the ground before the Ark of the Lord. *"Ah, Lord God!"* he cried out. *"Why have you brought this people across the Jordan at all, to hand us over to the Amorites so as to destroy us?"*[7]

The Lord said to Joshua, *"Stand up! Why have you fallen upon your face? Israel has sinned; they have transgressed my covenant that I imposed on them. They have taken some of the devoted things; they have stolen, they have acted deceitfully, and they have put them among their own belongings. Therefore the Israelites are unable to stand before their enemies."*[8]

The next morning Joshua rose early and made all the tribes pass before him. He was looking for the open door that evil was using to defile the entire congregation. After identifying the problem within the tribe of Judah, he made all the clans and families pass before him until he narrowed it down to one man named Achan.

"Give glory to God, my son," Joshua said. *"Make confession to him. Tell me now what you have done."*[9]

Achan answered, *"It is true; I am the one who sinned against the Lord God of Israel. This is what I did: when I saw among the spoil a beautiful mantle from Shinar, and two hundred shekels of silver, and a bar of gold weighing fifty shekels, then I coveted them and took them. They now lie hidden in the ground inside my tent, with the silver underneath."*[10]

After the Israelites identified the open door of sin and sealed it shut, they were able to proceed with God's plan. They marched into battle and defeated the kingdom of Ai. After assuming God's authority, with the help of the angelic warriors, they took possession over every place the soles of their feet tread.

The same concepts apply in the New Covenant. Just as the Israelites were given the authority to drive out their enemies, all spiritual warriors have been given the authority to drive out all forms of evil that violate their inner sanctuaries. When an intruder breaks in, like a thief in the night, all a warrior needs to do is turn on the lights and command the intruder to leave.

Every disciple of Christ has already been given the authority from Jesus. *I have given you authority to tread on snakes and scorpions, and over all the power of the enemy.*[11] All you need to do is address the demonic presence and speak the words, "I bind you, Satan, with the power and authority of the risen Lord Jesus Christ; and I command you into the abyss, never again to return!"

If the evil intruder doesn't leave, it means war. You will need to get your spirit-man fired up and send him into battle. In the same way the Israelites blew the ram's horn around the walls of Jericho, I usually begin the battle singing praise. Demons hate it when glory and praise is given to God.

Next, I search for an open door. I perform an inner diagnostic check to find out how evil has gained access to my inner sanctuary. I ask myself, how did I sin? Did something in my daily events trigger an emotional wound? Was I being passive in my worship to God? Many times the answers don't come easily. Demons don't want me to discover the doors they are using, and will do everything in their power to hinder my efforts.

In the same way Joshua made all the tribes pass before him until he discovered the weak link, many times I find it necessary to spend time in the Adoration Chapel until God shows me the problem. Other times I need to get away for a few hours and experience the joys of being in nature. Once I get my spirit-man back on line, I simply take authority over my spiritual house: "I bind you, Satan! Now get out of my house!" It is not the words that contain the power, but the strength of authority behind the words.

If for some reason the demons refuse to leave, I call down the heavenly host and have them destroyed. In the same way the Israelites were surrounded by angels in flaming chariots of fire, so every Christian is surrounded by holy warring angels of God.

In the spiritual realm it looks no different than the time Elisha and his servant found themselves surrounded by enemy troops. Elisha's servant was scared to death and said, *"Alas, master! What shall we do?"*[12]

Elisha replied, *"Do not be afraid, for there are more with us than there are with them." Then Elisha prayed: "O Lord, please open his eyes that he may see." So the Lord opened the eyes of the servant, and he saw; the mountain was full of horses and chariots of fire all around Elisha.*[13]

All Christians are surrounded by their guardian angels and each warrior has the right to call upon the heavenly host for assistance. In the same way the strong man called the local law enforcement agency to have the thieves arrested, all a warrior has to do is speak the words, "Lord Jesus, please send down warring angels to destroy anything demonic that's interfering with me!"

The Bible says all angels are ministering spirits *sent to serve for the sake of those who are to inherit salvation.*[14] Angels are servants who stand guard over all God's children day and night. The catechism says, *From its beginning until death, human life is surrounded by their*

*watchful care and intercession. Beside each believer stands
an angel as protector and shepherd leading him to life.
With their whole beings the angels are servants and messengers of God. Because they 'always behold the face of
my Father who is in heaven', they are the mighty ones who
do his word, hearkening to the voice of his word.*[15]

On two occasions, God allowed me to see my
guardian angel. Neither time could I see his face, much
less his shoulders. He towered over me like a mighty
skyscraper. I felt like I was standing next to a building
so tall that the top was concealed in the clouds. In
those moments I realized that nothing could harm me
outside of God's will.

When a demon violates my inner sanctuary and
doesn't obey my commands, all I have to do is judge it
as disobedient and sentence it to death. 1 Corinthians
6:3 says, *Do you not know that we are to judge angels —
to say nothing of ordinary matters?* If warriors are to
judge good angels, the same spiritual law applies to the
judgment of fallen angels.

With the power and authority that God has given
me to keep my spiritual sanctuary clean, I say to the
demons, "This is my circle of influence. There are no
trespassers allowed. I have given you a command;
because you have not obeyed my orders, I judge you as
disobedient, and sentence you to be destroyed in the
lake of fire."

Afterwards I ask Jesus, the Commander of the
Lord's Army, to send down an assignment of warring
angels and destroy all demons who have disobeyed my
orders, and to seal their remains in the lake of fire.

As God's child, it is my responsibility to pass along

my Father's judgments. God has already sentenced all demons to death. The Book of Revelation says that, their *time is short* and their place is in the *lake of fire.*[16] If I only cast the demons out of my circle of influence, they would hover in the near distance and wait for another opportunity to strike. Or worse, they might attack my ministry efforts, family members, or neighbors. When I pray to have the demons destroyed, it's like cleaning house. It wouldn't be right to take my trash and throw it in my neighbor's yard. Trash needs to be properly disposed of in the landfill, or in this case, the lake of fire.

Once a warrior learns how to take authority over his own inner sanctuary, he is ready to use the same principles to increase his circle-of-influence. In the same way the Israelites were sent to take authority over every place the soles of their feet tread, I learned how to take authority over my neighbor's property after buying a condemned house in northwest Denver.

Before I bought the house, it sat vacant for many years. All the windows were broken out and covered with plywood. The roof leaked, the hardwood floors were buckled from water damage, and a street gang had kicked open the back door. They had spray-painted all the walls with graffiti and were using the house as a drug hangout.

I started the renovation process with the exterior. I replaced the broken glass and started building a white picket fence in the front yard. A few days later, four gang members confronted me. I was working outside when two of them approached me from behind and the other two positioned themselves several inches away from my face.

"What are you doing here?" one of them asked.

"Building a fence. I'm also going to build a carport and plant sod in the front yard. Won't that look nice?" I said.

"What for? Why are you doing this?"

"I'm fixing the house so that a nice family can live here. Maybe when it's finished, your family can live here."

"Then you're a landlord!" he said.

"Yes, and that would make us neighbors. It's good to meet you. What's your name?"

"I'm the Viper," he said.

I extended my hand to shake his, but he and the others walked away. Afterwards I realized a battle had just been fought in the spiritual realm. It wasn't a physical battle where we threw punches, pulled knives, and shot guns. It was fought using the power of authority.

The gang members tried to intimidate me to see if I would back down or show signs of weakness. It didn't work. I continued to stand my ground and look them directly in the eyes. My spirit-man assumed the power and authority of ownership. In a language that transcended words I said, "This is my house! I will fight to protect my property! I will not be intimidated! I will never back down!"

When I returned the next day, one of the windows was broken. I ignored the problem in the physical realm and continued to fight the battle in the spiritual realm. I prayed that the Lord would send angels to watch over my property and for the Holy Spirit to convict the man who threw the rock. I asked the Holy Spirit to send a burning heat of conviction to lead the man in ways of righteousness for the salvation of his soul.

After praying about it for two weeks, I fixed the broken window and never had another problem with the street gang. My renovation efforts continued to flow smoothly until I realized the need to increase my circle of influence.

My neighbor's house was in terrible condition. It looked like it hadn't been painted in twenty years. White and aqua paint was curling off the southern side in large strips, showing the rotten wood underneath. I was concerned my neighbor's house would hinder the resale of my property, so one day I knocked on his door and said, "Hi, I'm your neighbor. What's your name?"

"I'm George. It's good to meet you."

"I'll be painting my house next week. I could bring over the airless and shoot yours too. How does $700 sound?"

"I know it needs work, but I can't afford it right now."

"$700 is a great deal. A house this size, you could expect bids from $2,000 on up."

"I'm sorry, but I can't afford it, you know — school and such."

After a long conversation, I walked away frustrated. His house looked terrible. It was going to hinder my property's resale. The fact that I couldn't do anything about the surrounding depravity made me feel powerless.

A few days later I went back and offered to paint his house for $400. He still couldn't afford it, so we settled on a free paint job. All George had to do was scrape off the old paint, and I would cover the rest.

A week later I knocked on George's door and asked why he hadn't scraped off the loose paint, and he said, "I tried sanding but it's too hard. Just paint it as is."

I gave my helper a push broom to rub off all the loose paint chips, while I masked off all his windows. After five hours, we painted everything a light cream color. George was overjoyed. His house looked a thousand times better, and afterwards, I realized the same dynamics apply to the spiritual realm.

Once a warrior renovates his own spiritual house, he can then increase his circle of influence to the surrounding areas. In the same way the strong man marked out the four corners of his property with stone towers, I increase the perimeter of protection surrounding my home with four rocks. I have anointed the rocks with oil and placed one in ever corner of my yard. Whenever I move, I take the rocks with me and pray for God to build a spiritual canopy of protection around my air space.

In the spiritual realm the canopy looks like a bullet-proof dome. I establish it with the principles of faith and ask the Lord to wash everything inside the canopy with his precious blood. I invite the Holy Spirit to dwell with me inside my spiritual canopy and ask God to assign warring angels to stand guard over me day and night. I pray the angels are given ongoing orders to strike down and destroy anything evil or demonic that enters the outer perimeter.

Once I have the canopy of protection built around my property, I maintain it on a regular basis. Just like Satan tempted Achan to open the door and bring stolen property into the Israelite camp, the presence of darkness is always trying to violate my air space. I have to run constant security checks and pray that God will seal up any breaches.

Unlike the strong man's situation, I don't invite thieves and robbers into my home unless it's for the express purpose of ministry. If a man is seeking spiritual direction or counseling, and he's submitting to my authority, then the authority of God who dwells in my house will cover him. If the man starts acting sinfully inside my house, mocking God and taking his name in vain and I keep silent, then in a way I am agreeing with him.

If I agree with the man and fail to take authority over the sin which I have invited inside my house, then my external barrier of protection has been breached. If on the other hand, I rebuke the man by saying, "Blessed be the name of the Lord! You shall not take the Lord's name in vain inside my house," then my canopy will remain intact.

Once I have my inner sanctuary glowing with the Holy Spirit and the perimeter of my property secure, I then use the same principles to advance my ministry efforts. Whenever I preach a sermon or conduct a seminar, I ask God to establish the same canopy of protection around the building where I'm speaking.

Like the Israelites, I take authority over every place where the soles of my feet tread. I drive out anything demonic and ask the Lord to wash the interior space with his blood. I pray for warring angels to be assigned to the entrance of the building, and to bind up anything demonic, in, on, or around the people who will be attending my seminars.

Without a protective canopy, most audiences will not be able to hear the gospel message because *the god of this world has blinded the minds of the unbelievers, to keep them from seeing the light of the gospel of the glory of Christ, who is the image of God.*[17] Without a spiritual canopy of protection, an angelic army to bind the demons and the power of the Holy Spirit to open men's hearts, most secular audiences will not be able to see the light of the gospel message.

When I work construction, I take authority over every place where the soles of my construction boots tread. I kneel down in the morning with the other workers and pray for angelic protection. I invite Jesus the carpenter to work beside me, and to anoint me with the power of the Holy Spirit. Whenever something evil interferes with the work of my hands, I take authority over the situation and call down the heavenly host.

In the same way, every warrior is required to take authority over every place where the soles of their feet tread. God has called every Christian to be priest, prophet, and king. The Catechism says, *"the laity are made to share in the priestly, prophetical, and kingly office of Christ. The whole People of God participates in these three offices of Christ and bears the responsibility for mission and service that flow from them."*[18]

A priest is a man who calls forth the power of God. Priests invite the presence of God into the Eucharist. They strengthen the assembly by preaching God's Word and they call upon the Holy Spirit to generate new birth at baptism. In the same way, all Catholics are called to bring God's presence and power into their circles of influence.

A prophet is a man who speaks the Word of God and delivers God's message. Prophets have the power to influence other men to make decisions for Christ. They speak words of truth and lead other men into a right relationship with God. Prophets have the power to work miracles and perform mighty signs and wonders. They bring God's light into a world of darkness.

A king is a man who rules over his kingdom. As God's children, we have become heirs to God's throne. When we inherit God's kingdom as adopted sons and daughters, God's kingdom becomes our kingdom. Every Catholic has been given the time, talents, power, authority, and responsibility to advance God's kingdom here on earth.

God has given his children dominion over all creation. He wants every warrior to take authority over every place where the soles of their feet tread. He has called every Catholic to be priest, prophet, and king. He wants his children to push back enemy lines, utilize the power of the angelic army, strike down anything demonic, and purge all evil from his kingdom. He has called every warrior into battle!

The Lord is with me like a dread warrior;
therefore my persecutors will stumble,
and they will not prevail.

Jeremiah 20:11

1

CHAPTER SIX

FULL ARMOR OF GOD

Several military transport ships approached the shore near Omaha Beach, Normandy. They were loaded with American soldiers wearing full combat attire. When the commander of the boat opened the steel door to let the men off near shore, a 50–caliber machine gun from the beach opened fire. Thousands of bullets cut through the troops, annihilating everyone in their path. Only a few men survived by jumping overboard, into the murky blood-red waters.

The sound system at the theater brought the scenes from *Saving Private Ryan* to life with dramatic effects. There were explosions, body parts lying on the beach, and wounded soldiers trying to take cover behind their fallen comrades.

As I watched the massacre, it made me angry at whoever was running the machine gun. Enemy troops were butchering innocent teenage boys who didn't look old enough to sign up for the draft. It reminded me of everyday life in the spiritual realm. All day long the enemy runs a 50-caliber machine gun loaded with fiery darts. Demons annihilate thousands of Christians every-day, and many of them don't know about the full armor of God.

Finally, be strong in the Lord and in the strength of his power. Put on the whole armor of God, so that you may be able to stand against the wiles of the devil. For our strug-gle is not against enemies of blood and flesh, but against the rulers, against the authorities, against the cosmic powers of this present darkness, against the spiritual forces of evil in the heavenly places.

Therefore take up the whole armor of God, so that you may be able to withstand on that evil day, and having done everything, to stand firm. Stand therefore, and fasten the belt of truth around your waist, and put on the breast-plate of righteousness. As shoes for your feet put on whatever will make you ready to proclaim the gospel of peace. With all of these, take the shield of faith, with which you will be able to quench all the flaming arrows of the evil one. Take the helmet of salvation, and the sword of the Spirit, which is the word of God.[2]

Now imagine the same combat scene, except this time picture the soldiers wearing the full armor of God. They look like knights with shiny armor. Their shiny steel plating is glowing with the power and presence of God. 50-caliber machine-gun fire bounces off of them like rubber darts hitting a concrete wall. After the sol-diers step off the transport ship and have a look around the beach, the lead man speaks one word and instantly the next bullet gets lodged in the machine gun's cham-ber. The next round explodes and eliminates the men-ace.

Before a warrior will be able to stand against the

wiles of the devil, he will need to put on the full armor of God. He will need to keep his spiritual force field charged at all times. He will need to fill himself with the power and presence of God. It takes a lot of current to stop bullets in midair. Without tapping into the spiritual energy available from the following sources, a warrior won't have the strength to stand against the wiles of the devil or tear down demonic strongholds.

Breastplate of Righteousness

The best defense against the whispering voice of temptation that leads men astray is the daily examination of conscience and the sacrament of Confession. Every time a warrior goes to Confession, even over the smallest of sins, he receives graces and power from God that add inches of steel plating to his armor.

Unfortunately, very few Catholics attend Confession these days. Out of the 3,000–family parish near my house, only fifteen people on average receive the sacrament of Reconciliation on Saturday afternoon. It's like that all across America. Catholics have bought into the same theologies that lead so many Protestants astray: "Why should I confess my sins to a priest when I can go directly to God?"

The Jews said the same thing to Jesus. *"Who can forgive sins but God alone?"*[3]

In response Jesus said, *"Why do you raise such questions in your hearts? Which is easier, to say to the paralytic, 'Your sins are forgiven,' or to say, 'Stand up and take your mat and walk'? But so that you may know that the Son of Man has authority on earth to forgive sins — he said to the paralytic — 'I say to you, stand up, take your mat and go to your home.'"*[4]

The power to forgive sins has passed from God the Father to Jesus. The question is, where did the power go from there?

When Jesus appeared to his disciples after his resurrection he said, *"As the Father has sent me, so I send you." When he had said this, he breathed on them and said to them, "Receive the Holy Spirit. If you forgive the sins of any, they are forgiven them; if you retain the sins of any, they are retained."*[5]

The power to forgive men's sins has been passed from Jesus to the apostles. The apostles passed the power on to their successors through *the laying on of hands.*[6] It began with Peter, the leader of the apostles and first Bishop of Rome, and has continued with an unbroken succession of Popes thereafter. The power has been passed through every bishop into all the priests through the laying on of hands for more than 2,000 years.

Confession is not an outdated practice; it's the system God set up for the forgiveness of sins. If you want to be forgiven, you need to make a sincere act of contrition and participate in the sacraments which God has ordained. In Confession, the penitent receives the grace necessary to close the door on evil, and keep his breastplate of righteousness shining with the purity of Christ himself.

Communion

One of the most powerful ways a warrior can

strengthen his spiritual armor is to receive the Divine Presence of God every day through Communion. Jesus says, *"Unless you eat the flesh of the Son of Man and drink his blood, you have no life in you. Those who eat my flesh and drink my blood abide in me, and I in them."*[7]

There's a difference between Protestant Communion and Catholic Communion. Most non-denominational churches serve Communion once a month. For them it is a symbolic remembrance of the Last Supper. The elements are no different from the bread and juice sold in the grocery store.

Catholic Communion is the actual presence of Christ. When the priest says the Eucharistic prayer, and the Church asks the Father to send his Holy Spirit on the bread and wine, they become the body and blood of Christ. Through the power of the Holy Spirit, Christ's sacrifice that was offered on the cross, is sacramentally made present to us through the Eucharistic.

Communion is my greatest source of strength. Without the daily nourishment of God's presence, I wouldn't have the ability to remove sin from my life or the anointing necessary for ministry.

I realized the prevailing force of this sacrament after spending a week on a houseboat at Lake Powell. I wanted to attend daily Mass, but because of the distance from the houseboat to the nearest church, it wasn't possible. During this time, I continued to pray and didn't notice any difference until I returned home and received Communion for the first time in a week. When I did, the presence of God flooded my soul. It brought tears to my eyes. I felt like the prodigal son when his father ran out to greet him with open arms. At that moment, I realized the Eucharist was the source and strength that makes my spiritual armor glow.

Adoration Chapel

In the Adoration Chapel a warrior can spend hours communing with the lover of his soul. Every time I walk into church and spend time in front of the Tabernacle, I walk out with God's anointing. It's through these quiet times that God speaks to me. When I practice contemplative prayer, I receive instructions and insights into the daily events surrounding my life. Sometimes God will show me his purpose and plans, other times he will bring up unhealed emotional wounds.

There was a time when I would shove my bad memories back down, but now that God has shown me how they are doorways that evil uses to access my inner sanctuary, I spend time working through the forgiveness process.

When the Lord brings a negative past experience to my attention, I will either write a love letter to the person who hurt me, or I will allow the memory to come alive in my imagination and ask God to guide me through the scene as I explore the feelings.

One memory started out in a large grocery store. There were endless rows of shelves, all of them towering to the ceiling. The little boy from my childhood, little Robbie, was all alone and terrified. Tears were streaming down his panic-stricken face. All the adults were pushing carts in a reckless scurry and ignoring him as if he were invisible.

As the images came alive in my imagination, I was able to enter the scene. I knelt down in front of the little boy and asked him, "What's wrong?"

"I... I... want my mommy," he said.

"I'll help you. Let's go find her."

He was traumatized and I could feel the same sick emotions. Now tears were streaming down both of our faces.

As we turned the corner, little Robbie caught sight of his mother. She was putting a bag of groceries into a cart. When we ran over to meet her, Robbie just wanted someone to hold him, but my mom looked as though she didn't care. Little Robbie needed his mother's love, but all I remember receiving was a lecture for wandering away in the first place.

I invited Jesus into the scene, and after taking little Robbie into my arms, I confronted my mother: "He was all alone and scared to death! Doesn't that matter to you?" I could tell she was burdened raising four kids and felt emotionally drained herself. She was doing the best she could.

After Jesus put his arms around my mother, her eyes filled with love. We were able to minister to little Robbie, and afterwards, I finished working my way through the forgiveness process.

As the scene came to a close, I realized it was one of the open doors evil had been using to drive my inappropriate behavior with women for many years. Demons had attached themselves to the unforgiving hurt and resentment toward my mother. Every time I entered a social situation, they would jab the wound and cause me to feel unloved.

I had a deep subconscious need to be loved by my mother and I had been trying to fill the void with women from the bar scene. I would go from one broken relationship to the next in the never-ending search for the perfect woman who could fill the gaping wound deep within my soul.

After I invited Jesus' love into my pain, I was able to forgive my mother. The doorway that evil was using to drive my inappropriate behavior was sealed shut. The divine presence of God filled the void within my soul and repaired the breach in my armor.

Belt of Truth

One of the fastest ways evil can enter a warrior's armor is to get him to believe a lie. One false belief can open a man up to a world of hurt. For example, I have heard many Catholics say, "Cancer is my cross to bear. It's God's will that I suffer. God must be punishing me."

God takes no pleasure watching demons attack and hurt his children. God allows suffering and even allows demons to attack people as a motivational force to get them to change their ways. Holiness and personal growth are pleasing to God, not pain, sickness, and suffering. The Bible gives us the following examples for the proper context of Christian suffering:

The first example comes from Timothy: *Indeed, all who want to live a godly life in Christ Jesus will be persecuted.*[8] When a man allows the light of Christ to shine brightly in a world of darkness, he will experience resistance in the form of persecution and suffering. But according to Matthew, the joys of righteousness should outweigh the pains of persecution. *Blessed are those who are persecuted for righteousness' sake, for theirs is the kingdom of heaven.*[9]

The second example comes from Hebrews: *Endure trials for the sake of discipline. God is treating you as children; for what child is there whom a parent does not discipline? If you do not have that discipline in which all children share, then you are illegitimate and not his children. Now, discipline always seems painful rather than pleasant at the time, but later it yields the peaceful fruit of righteousness to those who have been trained by it.*[10]

God allows his children to experience painful situations for the purpose of personal growth, holiness, and sanctification. In the bigger picture, it may be better a man suffer a terrible automobile accident, instead of losing his soul for all eternity. If a traumatic experience is the only thing that will cause a man to pursue God, then out of his great love, God will allow bad things to happen for the purpose of our own personal growth.

The third example comes from Galatians: *Live by the Spirit, I say, and do not gratify the desires of the flesh. For what the flesh desires is opposed to the Spirit, and what the Spirit desires is opposed to the flesh; for these are opposed to each other, to prevent you from doing what you want.*[11]

Christians are called to bring the desires of their flesh under control. Mortification is a process like fasting in which a man disciplines his body to get the desires of his flesh under control. When a man fasts, he is not punishing himself or inflicting pain on his body in an attempt to please God. Fasting is denying the physical need for food in exchange for spiritual food. When a man fasts, he converts all his fleshly hunger into spiritual hunger. When he cries out to God with spiritual hunger, God answers his cry and feeds him supernaturally.

By studying God's Word you will be better prepared to eliminate the enemy's lies from your thoughts. When the devil tries to convince you to suffer, you can rebuke his lies with God's truth. By doing so you will be adding another layer of protection to your spiritual armor.

Praise

When a warrior worships God, it puts a shiny coat of bullet-proof wax on his armor. Demons hate praise. It hurts their ears and makes them scurry like cockroaches in a dark room when the lights are turned on. It is especially powerful under the worst of circumstances.

I learned the power of praise late one night during a terrible storm. I moored my boat near shore and had to take shelter on the beach. About two in the morning, I woke up and took a flashlight to go check on the boat. It was still raining and I needed to turn on the bilge pump.

As I walked across the white, sandy shore, I came across an oar. I picked it up and said to myself, *this looks like the one I bought last week.* After walking a little farther, I came across a Tupperware container. It looked like the one I packed with the camping supplies.

I pointed the flashlight in the direction of the boat. It was gone. The storm had filled it to the point where it had capsized. My first reaction was shock and hopelessness. I was out there by myself in the middle of the night. All my equipment had either sunk or floated away.

As I waded through the bitterly cold waters in the dark, I started praising God. I didn't feel like praising God, but I did it anyway. Eventually, my negative attitude turned to pure joy. Whenever I found something, I carried it to shore singing, "Oh thank you, Great King, for saving the frying pan."

The next day, I was able to bail out the water and bring the boat to shore. Through the power of praise, I was able to turn what appeared to be a negative situation into a blessing. I didn't realize it at the time, but God was calling on me to part with the boat.

God always sees the bigger picture and deserves to be praised regardless of my limited perspective. Several weeks later, my insurance company covered the entire loss. I was able to recover all my personal property and I grew stronger from the experience through the power of praise.

Singing praises to God is more than watching the choir perform or making musical notes line up in perfect harmony. Authentic praise is where a warrior's spirit-man cries out to God with shouts of joy. When entire congregations come together to worship God in this manner, God shows up and moves in mighty ways. The power of praise will usher God's presence into the darkest of situations. It will add an impenetrable shield of protection to a warrior's armor and bring the light of

Christ into the most traumatic of situations.

The Helmet of Salvation

Every warrior needs an impenetrable helmet of pure thoughts. The battleground of the mind is extremely fierce. It's the first place evil attacks. Hundreds of thoughts run through a warrior's mind every hour. Thoughts in and of themselves can't hurt a man; it's only when he starts making agreements with negative thoughts that evil is able to influence his behaviors.

The ultimate condition for a warrior's mental purity comes from Philippians 4:8: *Whatever is true, whatever is honorable, whatever is just, whatever is pure, whatever is pleasing, whatever is commendable, if there is any excellence and if there is anything worthy of praise, think about these things.*

When demons continue to plague my thoughts with recurring temptations, I fight back using the same techniques that Jesus used in the wilderness. When Satan tempted him to turn stones into loaves of bread, Jesus fought back with the Word of God. He used a quote from the Old Testament and said, *"One does not live by bread alone, but by every word that comes from the mouth of God."* [12]

In the same way, whenever evil tries to tempt me with sexual thoughts, I fight back with the Word of God. I say to myself, "I am the bride of Christ, and I will keep myself pure and holy!" I keep repeating the phrase over and over again until the temptation subsides.

Other quotes that are extremely effective against the seductive whispering voice of evil are:

- God did not give me a spirit of fear, but love, power and self-control! (2 Timothy 1:7)

- Greater is He who is in me than he who is in the world! (1 John 4:4)

- No weapon fashioned against me will stand! (Isaiah 54:17)

The Word of God is a warrior's best defense against the seductive whispering of evil's temptations. It's an impenetrable shield that every warrior needs to keep his mental helmet shining brightly.

Combat Boots

As shoes for your feet, put on whatever will make you ready to proclaim the gospel of peace. When a warrior actively engages in ministry, God honors his efforts and gives him the spiritual strength he needs to love and serve the lost in this world. When a man sits at home and watches television, the spirit of God does not fill him with the miracle-working powers of Christ.

When I first started serving the homeless, I didn't have the strength or ability to be loving. I would start working with a homeless man in the morning, and after buying him clothes at a thrift store and driving him around to look for work all day, my loving intentions would be spent. By late afternoon, I would find myself cranky and impatient.

As I continued to push myself and stretch my abilities to be loving, God's love began to flow through me.

God started to fill my reservoir with an abundance of grace, patience, and wisdom that I needed to help the men overcome their drinking problems. In a lot of ways, I benefited more from God's anointing than the homeless men whom I was serving.

Unfortunately, very few Catholics feel qualified to perform acts of ministry. There seems to be a blanket of oppression that says, "Only an ordained priest is qualified to perform the works of God." There's also a stifling spirit that says, "All ministry must occur within the confines of the parish."

The Catechism says, *Lay people also fulfill their prophetic mission by evangelization, that is the proclamation of Christ by word and the testimony of life. To teach in order to lead others to faith is the task of every preacher and of each believer.*[13]

Every parishioner has been given the responsibility of evangelization. When a warrior starts proclaiming the gospel of peace, his spiritual armor will start to glow with the power and presence of Christ himself.

The Sword of the Spirit

The only offensive weapon is the sword of the Spirit. When a warrior speaks the Word of God, as defined in Sacred Scripture, he has the power to destroy strongholds, refute the enemy's lies, and bring love, healing, and unity into the lives of others.

Jesus says, *"If you continue in my word, you are truly my disciples; and you will know the truth, and the truth will make you free."*[14] When a warrior speaks the Word of God, as defined in Sacred Scripture, he is able to settle disagreements long before they turn into arguments. That's because *the word of God is living and active, sharper than any two-edged sword, piercing until it divides soul from spirit, joints from marrow; it is able to judge the thoughts and intentions of the heart.*[15]

During a radio interview, I was forced to use my sword when the host started condemning the Catholic Church's teaching on divorce and remarriage. I tried explaining the Church's position, but he didn't want to listen. The conversation was fast and furious. I don't remember the exact words, but I do know when I pulled out my sword. In response to his derogatory comments I said, "The Catholic Church is not based on what feels good. It doesn't bow down to public opinion or popularity. It is based on the Bible, and the Bible says with the exception of unchastity, the man who *marries a divorced woman commits adultery.*[16]

After I spoke God's truth into the situation, there were several seconds of dead silence over the airwaves. In the spirit realm, I took my sword and wounded the demon that was driving the man's anger. After that there was nothing left to say. The Word of God as defined in Sacred Scripture settled the debate.

Every warrior has been given a swift sword with unlimited power. Before he will be able to use it to refute the enemy's lies, he will need to feed himself on the Word of God every day. God wants to communicate with every man through Scripture and the only way a warrior will be able to strengthen himself is by reading the Holy Bible.

The Shield of Faith

One of a warrior's greatest strengths is the shield of faith. Not only will it quench the flaming arrows of the evil one, but it has the power to move mountains. Jesus says, *"If you have faith the size of a mustard seed, you will say to the mountain, 'Move from here to there,' and it will move; and nothing will be impossible for you."*[17]

Faith is more than an embodiment of religious doctrine, like when someone asks the question, "To what faith do you belong?" The answer is more than, "I belong to the Catholic faith," because faith is more than a collection of theological beliefs.

Faith is the instrument that a warrior uses to bring down the power of God into every situation that seems impossible.

For time would fail me to tell of Gideon,

Barak, Samson, Jephthah, of David and

Samuel and the prophets —

who through faith conquered kingdoms,

administered justice, obtained promises,

shut the mouths of lions, quenched raging fire,

escaped the edge of the sword, won strength

out of weakness, became mighty in war,

put foreign armies to flight.

Hebrews 11:32–34

CHAPTER SEVEN

A WARRIOR'S FAITH

Phase One Faith

At least four times in the Gospel of Matthew, Jesus challenges his disciples to increase their faith. Every time, he uses the term, "You of little faith." The first incident occurs right after the Sermon on the Mount when Jesus says, *"Do not worry about your life, what you will eat or what you will drink, or about your body, what you will wear. Is not life more than food, and the body more than clothing? But if God so clothes the grass of the field, which is alive today, and tomorrow is thrown into the oven, will he not much more clothe you – you of little faith?"[2]*

Before the disciples could trust Jesus to provide for their physical needs, they had to experience his sovereign power over their physical environment. After they watched him feed a crowd of five thousand with two loaves and five fish, they acquired phase-one faith.

Before I could trust God to provide for my physical needs, I also had to experience his sovereign hand. There was a season of my life when God allowed me to acquire a vast amount of money working in real estate. At one point, I thought I could retire. After a series of stock market losses, I went from a position of financial independence to having a few hundred dollars in my checking account.

At the time I was working with homeless men, driving them back and forth from detox, and helping them find jobs. Not only did this ministry consume most of my time, but it also cost a lot of money. Every month I was getting by on the bare minimum.

After about a year of living on complete dependence, I learned to trust God for my food, clothing, and shelter. It actually became fun at times, to see how God would provide for my needs. Every time a bill would come in the mail, I would also receive an unexpected blessing.

Eventually, I developed a sweet closeness with the Lord that I never had when I was financially independent. When I had the power of money, I didn't need the Lord to provide anything. I could buy, bribe, or negotiate my way through every kind of business deal imaginable. Before I could trust God with my finances, my spirit-man needed to cling to God for its very existence and survival. Afterwards, I developed phase-one faith.

Phase Two Faith

The disciples acquired phase-two faith on the Sea of Galilee. Shortly after they boarded a boat and pulled away from shore, Jesus fell asleep on a pile of fishing nets. As the disciples navigated their way toward the eastern shore, the gentle breeze turned into a nasty tempest. The sky grew dark and the waters grew turbulent. Soon whitecaps formed and threatened to tear the tiny craft apart. No one wanted to wake Jesus, but when the breakers came crashing over the hull, they ran to his side crying out, *"Lord, save us! We are perishing!"*[3]

Rising to his feet, Jesus rebuked the winds and the sea, and there was a dead calm. Turning to the disciples he said, *"Why are you afraid, you of little faith?"*[4]

The disciples were astonished. They whispered among themselves, *"What sort of man is this, that even the winds and the sea obey him?"*[5] One minute they were scared to death; the next, their eyes were opened.

Jesus didn't need to speak another word. The message was clear: Will you please just trust me! Nothing is outside my control. I have the ability to multiply loaves when you're hungry and rescue you from bodily harm when you're in danger.

Jesus allowed the situation to happen to teach the apostles a lesson. He could have prevented the storm in the first place. He could have rebuked the winds from his sleep without ever opening his eyes. Yet without the life-threatening experience, the apostles wouldn't have learned to trust the Lord with their lives.

I developed phase-two faith with a friend named Sandi. It was a warm spring morning in Golden, Colorado. After parking Sandi's car near the Coors brewery, we drove my truck up the road for several more miles. After finding the perfect spot, we strapped on our life jackets and launched our inflatable raft into the river.

We headed downstream for the ride of our lives.

The first few rapids spun us around backwards. We paddled hard to resume our position but before we could get straightened out, we hit more rocks and were swept through another series of rapids sideways.

"Huge drop-off, dead ahead," I called out.

It happened fast. Our raft took a vertical nose dive down a six-foot drop. White splashing waves thundered all around us. Sandi, who was in the back of the boat, couldn't hold on. She tumbled forward and knocked both of us into the water.

I could hear bubbles rushing over my ears; then only muffled silence. The freezing cold waters crushed my chest like a vise. I couldn't tell which way was up.

Suddenly I was at the surface. I could feel the warmth of Sandi's body against my legs six feet under. She was caught in the undertow. I could barely breathe, much less think. All I could do was raise one arm and grab the raft before it floated away. Helpless, I was swept downstream.

Jagged rock formations appeared from out of nowhere. The raging waters sent me crashing into them without mercy. I was scared to extend my feet out in front of me for fear my legs would be ripped off my body. I hit one massive boulder after another with devastating force.

My mouth was praying the entire time, but as soon as I started hitting rocks, my spirit kicked into high gear. I could hear my spirit-man crying out from inside of me with a one-word prayer, "God!"

Seconds later Sandi surfaced beside me and she was able to grab the raft. I climbed up her body like a ladder, and after spinning around, I pulled her inside. We lay in the bottom of the raft for several minutes trying to recover. When we looked up through the ever-changing water patterns that were splashing all around us, we realized God had worked another miracle. The raft had come to a complete stop in the middle of the river.

We were amazed. How does God stop a four-man inflatable raft in the middle of a river? There were large boulders and rushing waters all around us, yet we had come to a complete standstill. It took us a while to figure it out, but God sent an angel to cause the rope that was tied around the raft to get caught on something underwater.

Eventually, we were able to free the rope and paddle to shore using our hands. We walked away from the experience realizing the power of faith. It works like a beacon of light in a world of darkness. In the spiritual realm it looks like a porthole of light that God can use to send spiritual power into the physical realm.

Before the porthole could be established, several elements needed to be in place. First, we had to believe that God had the power and desire to rescue us from peril. We also had to believe that God is so closely connected that he knows every detail concerning our lives.

As soon as the situation grew dangerous, Sandi and I established a beacon of light into the heavenly realm through the power of faith when our spirits cried out to God. Once the spiritual connection was established, God was able to send forth his power and stop our raft in the middle of the river.

The opposite of faith is negativity, fear, and doubt.

As soon as Sandi knocked me into the water, I could have grown angry and started cursing. I could have spoken profanities and invited a spirit of negativity into the situation.

After crashing into the rocks, I could have fed into a spirit of despair with thoughts like, "I deserve this. God is punishing me. Bad things always happen to me. I'm going to die and no one cares." I could have made agreements with a spirit of fear, a paralyzing force that could have physically prevented me from grabbing hold of the raft.

Like a self-fulfilling prophesy, the cloud of darkness hovering over our situation could have grown much darker. After hitting a few more rocks, I could have started cursing God, taking his name in vain and wanting to die. If the inner thoughts of my spirit-man acted in this manner, or remained silenced by fear, the rafting experience could have ended in tragedy.

God in his great love would have wanted to save us, but if we had made agreements with evil, his hands would have been tied. God would not violate the spiritual laws of the universe and interfere with our free will.

Out of the three choices our spirits were given — silence, darkness, or establishing a spiritual pipeline through the power of faith — we chose to live. We cried out to God in our need, and the God of the universe calmed the river. We were able to walk away from the experience with a few bruises and a valuable gift. We acquired the ability to trust God with our lives.

Phase Three Faith

One day a man knelt before Jesus and said, *"Lord, have mercy on my son, for he is an epileptic and he suffers terribly; he often falls into the fire and often into the water. And I brought him to your disciples, but they could not cure him."*[6]

The young boy was surrounded by physicians, the apostles, and a large crowd of spectators. The apostles had already prayed over the boy. They tried to cast out the demon, but the doctors kept projecting negativity on the situation. They were making statements like, "There's no hope for this patient. It's impossible! All you can do is give the boy medications to make him feel better."

The father was also projecting negative faith. He had visited many doctors who diagnosed his son with epilepsy — a chronic nerve disorder of the brain affecting consciousness and muscular control.

Before Jesus could work a miracle, he needed to break the mental hold that the crowds had placed on the situation. He turned to the spectators and shattered their deception with a shocking statement, *"You faithless and perverse generation, how much longer must I be with you? How much longer must I put up with you? Bring him here to me."*[7]

Jesus could see the problem as clear as day. It was not a medical condition, just another demon. Jesus fired up his spirit, looked the demon in the eyes, and gave the command. Instantly, the boy was cured. Afterwards the disciples came to Jesus privately and asked, *"Why could we not cast it out?"*[8]

Jesus said to them, *"Because of your little faith. For truly I tell you, if you have faith the size of a mustard seed, you will say to this mountain, 'Move from here to there,' and it will move; and nothing will be impossible for you."*[9]

Jesus wanted his disciples to start using the power of faith. He wanted them to overcome the negative faith that was present in the crowd and open up a spiritual pipeline from heaven to earth. He wanted them to use the power of faith to work miracles. He wanted them to start moving mountains with the power of God.

Phase-three faith is a function of the spirit where a warrior starts cooperating with the power of God. Instead of asking God to do this and that, phase-three faith is where a warrior uses his own spirit, in cooperation with God's Spirit, and starts working miracles.

I started to develop phase-three faith after Mass one morning when an elderly lady named Betty approached me and said, "My granddaughter, Virginia, was arrested last night. She called collect and wants to use my house for bail. I was hoping she would call back, but she gets so angry. I would go visit her, but it takes two weeks."

"Two weeks! Did you call the jail and ask for visiting hours?"

"They only allow visits on Thursdays, but first I have to do the paperwork."

"No way! Attorneys make visits twenty-four hours a day. Just tell them you're with the church and you need to make a clergy visit."

"I can't do that; I'm so worried about her..."

The more Betty described the hopelessness of her

situation, the more empowered my spirit grew. I could feel the burning heat of God's spirit inside of me. I felt that I could walk through a brick wall and visit her granddaughter anytime I wanted. Without hesitation I said, "I'll stop by and visit her this afternoon."

"Oh, thank you so much," Betty said.

Later that afternoon, I pulled into the county jail's parking lot. Confidently, I approached two guards wearing dark blue uniforms. They were manning a security station behind bullet-proof glass.

"I'm here for a clergy visit," I said. "Her name is Virginia Brown."

Without saying a word, one of the guards took a clipboard and slid it through a steel drawer. After printing my name, I placed it back inside the drawer, stood to one side, and waited patiently.

After a few minutes, one of the guards left his post and was replaced by another. It looked like a shift change. After the second guard left, his replacement started screaming at me through the microphone. Looking the man directly in the eyes I said, "I'm here for a clergy visit."

He picked up the same clipboard and was about to pass it through the drawer when I stopped him by saying, "I'm already signed in." As the guard looked at my name, I moved to one side and continued to pray.

Soon a buzzer went off. The guard was motioning me through the steel door, so I pulled it open. On the other side, standing at the end of the hall, was a petite young lady wearing bright orange canvas pajamas.

"Are you Virginia?" I asked.

"Who are you?"

"I know Betty from morning Mass. She wanted me to come down and help you."

"How did you get in here?"

"I told them I was here to see you."

"That's so weird. I was just praying for help."

We both heard a banging noise on the glass behind us. When I turned around to look, the guard was waving at us with an impatient look on his face. He wanted us to enter the visiting room so that he could close the electronic door behind us.

After taking a seat on metal chairs, I offered Virginia the use of my cell phone.

"I still can't believe you got in here," she said.

After spending a half hour together talking and making calls, we concluded our visit in prayer. Virginia was able to make all the calls she needed and I was able to experience the power of phase-three faith. Through an unwavering mental belief and the strength of my inner spirit, I was able to cooperate with the miracle working power of God's Spirit. Without showing the guards any credentials, I was allowed a half hour visit with an unsupervised prisoner.

Phase Four Faith

Late one afternoon, Jesus wanted to go to the mountain by himself and pray. He made his disciples get into the boat and sent them ahead to the other side of the lake. *When evening came, he was there alone, but by this time the boat, battered by the waves, was far from the land, for the wind was against them.*[10]

Early in the morning, Jesus came walking toward them on the water. The disciples were still a long way from shore. When they looked to the horizon, they saw the figure of a man approaching them from the distance. They were terrified and said to one another, *"It is a ghost!"*[11]

Immediately, Jesus spoke to them saying, *"Take heart, it is I; do not be afraid."*[12]

Peter answered him, *"Lord if it is you, command me to come to you on the water."*[13]

Jesus said, *"Come."*[14]

So Peter got out of the boat, started walking on the water, and came toward Jesus. But when he noticed the strong wind, he became frightened, and beginning to sink, he cried out, "Lord, save me!"[15]

Jesus immediately reached out his hand and caught him, saying to him, "You of little faith, why did you doubt?" When they got into the boat, the wind ceased. And those in the boat worshiped him, saying, "Truly you are the Son of God."[16]

I'm sure Peter could feel the negativity being projected upon him by the other disciples. They were probably smirking or making comments like, "Get back in the boat before you drown. No one can walk on water. It's impossible!" Yet Peter stepped out of the boat and established phase-four faith — power over his physical environment.

Peter knew Jesus had power over the sea and he also trusted Jesus with his life. He had been given the power to cast out demons and heal people, so why not climb out of the boat? Being a fisherman, he spent most of his life on the sea, developing a feel for the rhythm of the waves, and a respect for the current's power. Now the test had come — could he control his thoughts long enough to walk on water?

Every time I try walking across a small puddle, my thoughts start screaming negative words of condemnation, "You can't do that!" I can feel the doubt rising up in my heart before my foot touches the water's edge. I have never been able to walk on water, but I have been given power over my physical environment. Whenever I work construction, I use my body, mind, and spirit to manipulate and change my environment.

Some construction workers project a negative spirit over their work. They are always cursing and breaking things. Other construction workers have an anointed flow. They use their inner spirits to create a peaceful flow in their work. All the cuts they make seem to fit together perfectly, as their work becomes a form of art.

Other men try to work with their hands but they never involve their spirits. They buy how-to books and approach tasks from an intellectual perspective. With enough persistence they can finish a job, but without involving their spirits, they will never acquire the anointed flow that is required to work miracles.

I started experiencing the power of phase-four faith the day I volunteered to remove a chandelier for the Cathedral of the Immaculate Conception. It was installed during the 1970s, when a need arose for more lights to televise a Mass for shut-ins. A team of engineers designed a gold chandelier which was suspended above the altar by four square posts. It was 50 feet wide, 60 feet tall, weighed 2,000 pounds, and had eight light compartments that looked like 55-gallon barrels.

The director of the Cathedral hated it. He said the modernist style from the 1970s conflicted with the white, Gothic, upward flow of the Cathedral's original design. He wanted to remove it, but architects told him the job would take two weeks, cost $30,000, and need 80 feet of scaffolding.

When he approached me with the idea, I said, "I'll have it down in a day. It won't cost you anything and I'll even patch the ceiling from the attic without scaffolding." Something in my spirit knew it was possible. I didn't even stop to think the job through; I just rounded up three other guys one Saturday morning.

We started the process by turning on the winch that was set up in the attic. It was designed to lower the chandelier to within reach of a ladder so that the maintenance man could change lightbulbs. After letting the winch down all the way, we started taking the contraption apart. Within an hour we had removed everything but the four steel posts that were protruding from the ceiling. They were dangling from the winch cables about ten feet above the floor.

To get the first one down, I needed Bart and Chad to hold the end of the post near the altar steps. After Tim, who was up in the attic, cut the cable, I was going to guide the post down the center aisle. I had nailed together several two-by-fours that I was going to use to guide the forty-foot-long post safely between the rows of pews.

As soon as Tim cut the cable, the end of it snapped down toward Bart and Chad like a bull whip. The cable was moving so fast that we could hear it cutting through the air but could barely follow it with our eyes. Once the cable reached the end of its pendulum swing, it started heading back toward Bart and Chad for another pass.

I continued to scream, "Hold it! Hold it!" but they had forgotten all about holding the end of the 500-pound post.

I chased after the post with my two-by-four screaming, "No! No!" but it was too late. The post was headed straight for the wooden pews. As soon as it snapped the two-by-four into pieces, my spirit-man took control. The forty-foot-long post came crashing down with a thundering boom.

It was so loud that the Director heard the noise from the rectory and came running through the door screaming, "What happened? What happened?"

Bart and Chad were so shaken up they could barely talk. "Everything's fine," I said. "We just lowered the first post. See? A perfect landing, right down the center aisle."

By every law of physics, the post was headed straight for the pews. It should have landed on them and crushed them, but miraculously, through the power of faith and the persistent force of my spirit-man, the physical surroundings yielded to the spiritual power of God. The Lord worked a miracle and saved the first five rows of pews from being shattered into toothpicks.

In phase one and two, the warrior learns to trust God, not with an intellectual belief, but with his spirit. The warrior's spirit-man learns to trust the Father's

Spirit. The two spirits start to develop a sweet closeness and connection. A bond is formed that allows a warrior to cry, "Abba Father!"

In phase three and four, the warrior starts using his spirit in connection with God's Spirit to work miracles. The two spirits are joined together. The miracle-working power of God's Spirit begins to flow through the warrior's spirit. The two spirits become one.

CHAPTER EIGHT

A WARRIOR'S LOVE

One day God gave me an extremely difficult assign-ment. He sent me to help a homeless man named Steven who had set up camp in the bushes alongside the Platte River. When I first met Steven, he suffered from malnutrition, had festering cuts on his hands, and hadn't bathed or changed clothes in weeks. Every night he would pass out drunk in a pile of carpet scraps that were rolled up in the bushes.

At first Steven didn't trust me. I would stop by and visit him two or three times a week. Some days I would bring a box of fried chicken or sandwiches for dinner; other days I would sit on broken pieces of concrete near the river and listen to his stories. It took a while, but eventually we developed a friendship.

It turns out Steven had been a lieutenant command-er with the Navy Seals. He had fought in Vietnam and volunteered to stay three more years to go on a killing spree and get even for all the men he had lost in his pla-toon. He had suffered an extremely abusive childhood. His father would beat him bloody, and afterwards he would pick himself up off the floor and dare his father to hit him again.

My assignment was to rescue Steven from the clutches of evil and deliver him back to his heavenly Father who loved him. Steven was a lost sheep wandering in the wastelands of eternal destruction. He was immersed in sin, ensnared in a fornication relationship with a neighboring camp's prostitute, and was full of hate toward all humanity. Yet God loved him and wanted him back in the flock; clean, sober, singing praises, and worshiping him in spirit and truth.

I went into the battle wearing the full armor of God. I proceeded with the power of faith knowing God had a purpose and plan or else he wouldn't have called me into action. I continued to use the power of prayer, even though I felt God's hands were tied, because no one could force Steven to change his behavior and stop drinking. He had to make that choice himself.

I used my sword to fight the lies and speak God's truth into his life every chance I got, but Steven had a sword too. He knew the Bible, or as least his version of the Bible. He was a graduate from theological seminary and was the most argumentative and contentious man I had ever met. We would get in major "sword fights" over religion. When I confronted him with scriptures on drinking, he would defend his behavior with statements like, "Jesus drank wine. He got everyone drunk at the wedding feast at Cana."

I was using the power of warfare prayers, but there wasn't any way for me to take authority over the demons that were driving his drinking problem. They had a right to be there because every time Steven would take a drink, he was saying yes to the devil and no to God. They had direct access to his mind and emotions. I could lay hands on him and command all demons to flee, but they would come right back again the next time he wanted to drink.

The only way I could help Steven was through the power of love. Love has the ability to cut through darkness like the light of day. Love softens the hardest of hearts. When a warrior taps into God's love and channels it into the lives of others, miracles start to happen.

When I looked at Steven through the eyes of God's love, I began to see his pain. He suffered tremendously. The voices and faces of the men he killed in Vietnam haunted him night and day. Memories of his father beating him and locking him in the cellar continued to wound him deeply. Steven's spirit-man was tormented by demons, and his inner sanctuary was filled with rage.

God wanted to rush into Steven's heart and comfort his pain, but Steven didn't allow anyone near his heart. It was severely wounded and heavily guarded. There was no way to break through unless Steven lowered some of his defense mechanisms.

I started using the power of love every time I stopped by the river and brought him something to eat. I fed his physical body with food and his hungry soul with love. When he accepted my gifts of love, he was also accepting God, because God is love. Every time we ate a chicken dinner together, a small amount of God's light would enter his world of darkness.

As soon as it did, the demons would throw fits. They fought back by filling his mind with all kinds of perverted thoughts regarding my intentions. Demons hate love because they are defenseless against love's power to transform lives. As soon as Steven allowed a small amount of God's love into his soul, it cut both ways. For a short time it made him feel better, but it also reminded him of the amount of misery that surrounded his life.

The more I tapped into God's love, the more I could feel God trying to get inside of Steven's heart. When I looked at the wounds on his hands, I knew God could feel his pain too. When I connected with God's love, it prompted me to say, "Let's go to the store and get some bandages for your hands."

"I don't need any bandages," Steven said.

"It hurts me just looking at your hands. What happened? How did they get so infected?"

After looking at his hands for a long time, Steven began to connect with his pain. I could also feel God's love flowing through me as it started to awaken a hurt deep within his heart.

"I don't need bandages. On the front lines we glued our wounds together. Pain is for sissies."

"I'm heading to the store. We could stop by the deli for lunch and pick up a few medical supplies," I said.

Eventually, Steven broke down. We went to the store and he allowed me to minister to his wounds. When he did, he accepted even more of God's love into his heart.

As the months continued, the amount of God's love that entered Steven's heart had grown to the point where he was starting to despise his living conditions.

He began to see himself differently. When Steven was consumed in self-hate, he didn't mind sleeping in the bushes. The more love he accepted, the less he wanted to subject himself to inhumane conditions.

Eventually one day he broke down and said, "I don't want to die out here. Will you help me get off the ground?"

"Sure, I already called detox. After you get sober, I will help you find a job and a place to stay."

Later that afternoon we packed up his belongings and I drove him to the detox facility. On his second day he experienced a massive seizure and almost died. The head nurse called the paramedics and he was transported to a hospital where he remained for three more days. After they released him, his contentious personality was gone, and the only thing that remained was the broken, empty shell of a man.

I let him stay at my house for a few days until he was feeling better. Afterwards we found a studio apartment and I paid his first month's rent and the security deposit. He started looking for work by walking around the neighborhood. Within a few days, he found a job painting a house.

Everything appeared to be going fine until payday. After cashing his check, he spent $200 on beer and threw a party for all his neighbors. Later that week he was evicted and living back in the bushes alongside the Platte River.

I wanted to cuss him out for trashing the apartment, but after looking into his eyes, God's love flooded my soul. Relentlessly, God pursued Steven. Not only had

God forgiven him, but God was pushing me to continue my efforts in helping him.

It took several more months, but eventually Steven grew tired of sleeping on the ground. He missed the comforts of his own apartment. Once again I agreed to help, except this time, I refused to pay more than $35 to rent a bunk at a Working Man's Shelter.

After he was released from detox, he spent one night in the shelter before moving back to the river. He camped there for almost a week and still maintained his sobriety. After finding a job at an aluminum-can recycling plant, his employer let him sleep on the floor at night until he had saved enough money to rent another apartment.

Every time I stopped by his new place to visit, he had acquired more furniture. On the weekends he would collect aluminum cans and search through dumpsters for things that he used to decorate his new home. We started praying together, and even though we would get into theological arguments, they were more on a respectful basis. He even began telling me stories from his past when he first became a Christian.

Everything was going great until the Fourth-of-July weekend arrived and he asked himself, "What's wrong with having just one drink?" Well, one drink turned into a three-week binge and he lost his job, his apartment, and all his new belongings. He repeated the same cycle and ended up back on the Platte River. However, this time it didn't take him as long to get back on his feet. After spending several weeks on the ground, he was ready to give it another try.

Over the next twelve months, Steven lost his sobriety on several more occasions, and every time God relentlessly pursued his beloved child. Steven made so much progress that the last time he took a drink, he explained the situation to his employer and asked to have a few days to check himself into detox. His employer agreed and he was able to keep his job and pay the rent, without losing anything.

One of the most loving moments we shared together occurred right before Christmas. We were talking on the phone and I was trying to get inside his heart. The compelling force of God still wanted to get deeper inside of Steven's emotional wounds, and as I entered that sacred space, I could feel his loneliness.

"What do your holiday plans look like?" I asked.

"My boss gave all the pack-builders a $200 bonus and a twenty-pound turkey. I didn't have any way to cook mine, so I gave it to one of the guys."

"Would you like to spend Christmas with my family? We could go to church in the morning and have turkey dinner afterwards."

There was a long period of silence on the phone before he said, "You would do that for me?"

"Sure, it will be great! I'll pick you up around eleven a.m."

A few minutes later Steven tried to start a fight with me over what church we would attend. I told him it didn't matter and that we could go to any church he wanted, but he kept making remarks like, "The Bible says, call no man your father."

"Please come to dinner with my family. I don't want to get into another argument over religion."

The love I had extended Steven stabbed deep within his heart and uprooted more emotional wounds. The demons who had access to those wounds were throwing a fit. He desperately wanted to be loved, yet as a defense mechanism, he tried to start another argument.

Eventually, Steven started cussing at me and calling me names. It got so bad I had to hang up. He called back five minutes later even angrier. This time he started attacking my character, "You're just a rich yuppie. You have no idea what it's like living on the streets. You couldn't survive a second out here."

When he started using profanities, I unplugged the phone and took the matter to the Lord: "I don't need this abuse. I have been nothing but good to him and now he's cursing at me."

Relentlessly, God continued to pursue Steven. In my prayer time God gave me the strength to love even in the face of his abuse. I went to the store and bought Steven a set of barbells for Christmas. I knew he wanted a set because as a Navy Seal, he used to be in excellent shape. After the years of alcohol abuse had taken their toll on his body, he wanted to start working out again.

Early the next morning I knocked on his door to deliver the present. Once again the power of love flooded his heart. He was overjoyed. The present almost made him cry. He said, "I don't say this to anyone but, I, I love you, man."

"I love you too, Steven."

Over the years I watched the power of love deliver Steven from the jaws of death. Love transformed an angry, raging alcoholic into a godly man who now spends his time helping other homeless men and women rise above the streets.

What a tremendous privilege it is for Catholic warriors to take the power of God's love into the hearts of those who have been hurt. Love is a spiritual power that helps wounded men and women rise to their feet. It pays the price for another man's sins, so that the power of God can enter his heart and begin the conversion process. Love will break through the most difficult of strongholds and deliver those who are lost in darkness.

Another example of love's power to overcome evil comes from the life of Richard Wurmbrand.[2] He was a Romanian evangelical pastor who suffered fourteen years of persecution in a Communist prison camp for his faith. After his release, he wrote several books that describe his encounter with some of the worst acts of persecution imaginable.

In one of his stories, Richard describes a time when everybody received twenty-five lashes for playing a game of chess with figures they had made out of pieces of bread. Richard was fastened to a concrete wall with chains. His arms and legs were spread apart as his bare back absorbed the cruelty of the whip. After a severe beating, several guards threw his limp body into an isolation cell.

Instead of allowing a spirit of anger or retaliation to drive him insane, he used the power of love to overcome his pain. He forced his body off the floor and went to the other bunk to help his friend Gaston who was lying face down. He too had been severely beaten.

Tearing a small piece of cloth from his shirt and

soaking it in water, he ministered to Gaston's wounds and examined the torn flesh for splinters of wood. Gaston's body shook as with a fever. He could barely speak.

The only prisoners who survived such abuse were those who used the power of love. Men who allowed themselves to feed into their angry emotions were quickly consumed by the spirit of evil that hovered over the camp. Not only were men like Richard able to protect themselves with the power of love, but they also used it to advance the kingdom of God.

In another camp a woman named Ann Marie was arrested for her work in the underground church.[3] Like the others, she was beaten and tortured to make her betray the names of those involved in her ministry. During one of her sessions she said to the man who was holding the chains in his hand, "You beat me in vain! You will never beat out of me my love for God, nor my love for you."

The torturer laughed and said, "What a foolish girl you are! I beat you and you declare your love for me."

"I will now tell you words that under normal circumstances you would never hear from a girl. While you beat me, I look at your hands. How beautiful they are! I imagine how your wife enjoys it when you caress her. I put to you a simple question: is caressing not better than beating? When you caress your wife, you and she have pleasure. You surely cannot enjoy torturing more than caressing.

"You have very attractive lips. How your wife must have rejoiced when you first kissed her. Is kissing not better than swearing at people and cursing with foul words?"

He slapped her in the face and said, "Stop this stupid talk! I'm not interested in your idiotic lies. You'd better tell us with whom you worked in your underground activity. We are not in the business of love here, but in discovering counter-revolutionist activities."

She responded, "I have a boyfriend who not only loves me — he is love itself. From him I have learned to love everyone. I love those who do me good. I love those who hurt me."

He gave her a blow. She fell to the concrete floor, hit her temple, and fainted. When she awoke, she saw the torturer sitting deep in meditation.

"You prisoners shout when you are beaten. Why? You feel pain, but what is your suffering compared with mine? You get beaten at most for half an hour. We have to beat so many. There is not time for more than that. Then you rest in your cell. But I have to beat eight hours a day. I have done this six days a week, twelve months a year, for ten years. The only music I hear is the noise of the whip and the cries of the tortured. It is maddening. In the evening I get drunk and then go home, where I beat my wife, too."

After a brief moment of silence he asked her, "Who is this strange boyfriend of yours who taught you to love both the good and the bad without distinction?"

She told him, "It is Jesus," and she spoke to the torturer about him.

"How can I become his friend too?" he asked.

"You must repent of your sins, put your faith in his dying for you on the cross, and be baptized."

"Then baptize me," he demanded. Dragging her to a pool, he threw her into the water, and she baptized him. It was a sincere conversion. The proof was that at great risk to himself he succeeded in setting her free.

Another example of love comes from a small town in the Midwest where a large turntable bridge spanned a great river.[4] During most of the day, the bridge was set with its length running parallel to the banks of the river to allow ships to pass freely on either side. During certain times of the day, the bridge needed to be turned sideways to allow a train to cross the river.

A switchman sat in a small shack to operate the controls for the bridge and lock it into position whenever a train needed to pass. One evening the switchman was waiting for the last train of the day. He looked into the distance and caught sight of the train's light. He stepped to the controls and pulled back on a large lever. To his horror the locking mechanism didn't engage. If the bridge was not securely locked in position, it would wobble back and forth at the ends, causing the train to jump the track and crash into the river below.

Immediately he rushed across the bridge to the other side where there was another lever that could be used to operate the lock manually. Upon reaching the lever, he pulled back on it with all his might. He could feel the rumble of the train vibrating the tracks beneath his feet. He leaned backward to apply all his weight to it, locking the bridge into position. Many lives depended on this man's strength to keep enough pressure on it until the train had passed.

From across the bridge, in the direction of the control shack, he heard a sound that made his blood run cold: "Daddy, where are you?" His four-year-old son was crossing the bridge to look for him. His first impulse was to cry out to the child, "Run! Run!" But the train was too close. The boy's tiny legs would never make it across the bridge in time. The man almost left the lever to run and grab his son and carry him to safety, but he realized he could not get back to the lever in time. Either the people on the train or his son had to die. It only took a moment for him to make the decision.

The train sped swiftly and safely on its way. No one on board was even aware of the tiny, broken body thrown mercilessly into the river. Nor were they aware of the pitiful figure of a sobbing man still clinging tightly to the locking lever long after the train had passed. They didn't see him walking home slower than he had ever walked before to tell his wife how he had sacrificed their son.

The most profound definition of love occurred at Golgotha where the wooden cross fell to the ground and Jesus' broken body was thrown down upon it backwards. Several guards held his arms and legs as the centurion drove wrought-iron spikes through his wrists. They pressed his feet together, toes pointing down, and drove another spike through the arch of his feet.

The sound of metal striking metal spurred the angry crowd into furious rage. They mocked him with statements like, "He saved others, but he can't save himself. The King of the Jews — ha! Let him come down from the cross and rule over Israel."

After the cross was raised, great waves of pain swept over his muscles, knotting them in relentless, throbbing cramps. The full weight of his body was suspended from the wrought-iron spikes. He was unable to breathe without pulling himself upward. To bring in the smallest amount of life-giving oxygen into his lungs, Jesus had to pull against the steel spikes. With every breath he took, more tissue was ripped from his already lacerated backside as it scraped against the rough wood of the cross.

After hours of relentless, throbbing pain, carbon dioxide began to fill his lungs and poison his bloodstream. The muscles of his heart were struggling to pump thick, sluggish blood into his tissues. He could feel the chill of death creeping into his body as the crowd kept shouting profanities, throwing rocks, and mocking him. "This man claimed to be God. He wanted to destroy our temple and rebuild it in three days."

With one last surge of strength, Jesus looked into the eyes of the men who surrounded him and with love in his heart, he pressed against the nails to bring in enough air to utter the words, *"Father, forgive them; for they do not know what they are doing."*[5]

Instantly, the curtain in the temple was torn in two, the earth shook, and rocks were split apart. The tombs of the just were opened and many bodies of the saints who had died were raised. Jesus conquered evil through the power of love. In that moment, he opened up a spiritual conduit between heaven and earth. He took all the sickness Satan could inflict upon him and remained loving.

Jesus defeated evil through the power of love.

Before the Crucifixion, Satan and his vast army of demons had successfully covered the entire world with darkness. It started with the fall of Adam and Eve and continued through every generation. To break through the cloud of darkness, Jesus became a man. He veiled his divinity and took the form of a slave. He entered the world of darkness to establish a spiritual pipeline of God's love from heaven to earth.

Now every warrior can tap into the same spiritual pipeline of God's love. A warrior can walk into the darkest pit of hell, whether it be a night club, a prison cell, or a concentration camp and disburse the darkness by connecting to the pipeline that Jesus established on the cross. When a warrior is loving, God's love flows through the man and dispels darkness just like a lamp in a dark room.

Love is more than an emotion. It is a spiritual function of the heart. Feelings come and go. Christ didn't feel like dying on the cross. He begged the Father, *"If it is possible, let this cup pass from me; yet not what I want but what you want."*[6] Jesus made the choice of love. He made a decision to suffer the cruelty of Satan's sickness to establish the New Covenant.

Love is an active struggle against evil. It is not a passive state of tolerance that suffers abuse. Love stands up for what is right regardless of the cost. Love desperately desires to get inside of everybody's heart. It wants to fill every man's inner sanctuary with the light of hope and affirm everything that is good. Love brings out our best qualities. It looks past external behaviors and brings out every man's true potential.

God is love and love conquers all. A warrior's number-one weapon against evil is love. With the power of love, warriors will be able to set captives free, heal the broken hearted, crush demonic strongholds, and bring the light of Christ into a world of darkness. Love heals all wounds, it restores broken marriages, it softens the hardest of hearts, it bears all things, it believes all things, it endures all things. Love conquers all!

All authority in heaven and on earth
has been given to me. Go therefore and
make disciples of all nations,
baptizing them in the name of the
Father and of the Son and of the Holy Spirit,
and teaching them to obey
everything that I have commanded you.

Matthew 28:18–20

CHAPTER NINE

THE COMMISSIONING

You are hereby commissioned to go forth and advance the kingdom of God. The Commander of the Lord's army says, "Go forth! The time is short." Go forth and wage war against all forms of evil that have infiltrated your sphere of influence. Go forth and take authority over every place where the soles of your feet tread. Go forth and produce everlasting fruit with the talents and abilities that you have been given.

As a spiritual warrior, you have been given the power of faith. You can say to the mulberry tree, *be uprooted and planted in the sea, and it would obey you.*[2] Jesus says, *"For truly I tell you, if you have faith the size of a mustard seed, you will say to this mountain, 'Move from here to there,' and it will move; and nothing will be impossible for you."*[3]

You have the power of love. You can use it to soften hardened hearts, restore broken marriages, raise godly children, comfort the lonely, and heal emotional wounds. God is love, and by tapping into God's endless supply, you can bring the power of God into the darkest pits of hell, whether it's a nightclub, a prison cell, or a concentration camp.

You have been given the full armor of God and the power to stand against the wiles of the devil. You have the belt of truth, the breastplate of righteousness and the gospel of peace for your feet. You have a shield of faith to quench all the flaming arrows of the evil one. You have the helmet of salvation and the sword of the spirit, which is the Word of God.

You have the power of prayer. You can go boldly before the throne of grace anytime you want. Jesus says, *"I will do whatever you ask in my name, so that the Father may be glorified in the Son. If in my name you ask me for anything, I will do it."*[4]

You have been given authority over all the works of the enemy. Jesus gave the power to all his disciples when he said, *"I watched Satan fall from heaven like a flash of lightning. See, I have given you authority to tread on snakes and scorpions, and over all the power of the enemy; and nothing will hurt you."*[5]

You have been given the power of the heavenly host. *Beside each believer stands an angel as protector and shepherd leading him to life. With their whole beings the angels are servants and messengers of God. Because they 'always behold the face of my Father who is in heaven', they are the mighty ones who do his word, hearkening to the voice of his word.*[6]

You have been given the covering of a worldwide Church. It was founded on Peter the day Christ said, *"You are Peter, and on this rock I will build my church, and the gates of Hades will not prevail against it. I will give you the keys of the kingdom of heaven, and whatever you bind on earth will be bound in heaven, and whatever you loose on earth will be loosed in heaven."[7]*

You have been given the assurance of a worldwide Church. The keys of the kingdom of heaven represent power and authority that was given to Peter. He was the leader of the twelve apostles, and when he died, he passed the keys on to Saint Linus who became the second Pope — Bishop of Rome. When Saint Linus died, he passed the power and authority on to Saint Anacletus, and the succession of Popes has continued from there, for more than 2,000 years.

You have been given the protection of a worldwide Church. The Catholic Church has lasted longer than any government in the world. It has the protection of Christ's promise when he said, *"The gates of Hades will not prevail against it."[8]* The Catholic Church will continue in existence until the end of time.

You have the power of Holy Communion. You can receive the Divine Presence of God every day. It is more than a symbol; it is the actual presence of Christ. Jesus says, *"Unless you eat the flesh of the Son of Man and drink his blood, you have no life in you."[9]* Communion is life-giving food that will nourish and renew your spiritual life in the same way that material food nourishes your body.

You have the power of Confession. You can have your sins washed away anytime you want. As far as the east is from the west, God will remove your sinfulness. Through the sacrament of Confession, you will be reunited with Christ. You will receive the necessary graces to remove sins from your life.

You have the fellowship and communion with more than a billion Catholics worldwide. Anywhere you go in the world, from the smallest village in Africa to the great city of Rome, there's a Catholic church nearby. You can have fellowship with the community of believers, who all agree upon the same doctrine and who all acknowledge the supremacy of the Papacy. You can connect to your spiritual family anytime you want and receive the necessary support and encouragement to strengthen your spiritual journey.

You have the richness and depth of 2,000 years of Church history. You can receive wisdom and insight from hundreds of holy men and women of God who have founded the Church by their godly examples and have advanced it through the price of their own blood. St. John of the Cross, St. Thomas Aquinas, St. Augustine, St. John Chrysostom, St. Teresa of Avila, St. Catherine of Siena, and St. Francis de Sales have all left behind incredible writings and the godly examples of their own lives.

You have been given the Holy Bible. You can commune with God anytime you want simply by reading his Word. *The word of God is living and active, sharper than any two-edged sword, piercing until it divides soul from spirit, joints from marrow; it is able to judge the thoughts and intentions of the heart.*[10] By mediating on God's Word, you will be able to renew your mind daily in Christ Jesus.

You have been given the Catechism of the Catholic Church. It is a profoundly deep and most beautiful collection of writings about the faith. There are 2,865 sections that *faithfully and systematically present the teach-*

ing of Sacred Scripture, the living Tradition in the Church and the authentic Magisterium, as well as the spiritual heritage of the Fathers, Doctors, and saints of the Church.[11]

You have been given the power of the Holy Spirit at baptism when your soul was imprinted with an indelible spiritual sign. *Baptism not only purifies from all sins, but also makes the neophyte "a new creature," an adopted son of God, who has become a "partaker of the divine nature," member of Christ and co-heir with him, and a temple of the Holy Spirit.[12]*

You have been given the power of the Holy Spirit at confirmation when your soul was imprinted with an indelible character. *Confirmation brings an increase and deepening of baptismal grace: it unites us more firmly to Christ; it increases the gifts of the Holy Spirit in us; it renders our bond with the Church more perfect; it gives us a special strength of the Holy Spirit to spread and defend the faith by word and action as true witnesses of Christ, to confess the name of Christ boldly, and never to be ashamed of the Cross.[13]*

You have been given the gifts of the Holy Spirit. *To one is given through the Spirit the utterance of wisdom, and to another the utterance of knowledge according to the same Spirit, to another faith by the same Spirit, to another gifts of healing by the one Spirit, to another the working of miracles, to another prophecy, to another the discernment of spirits, to another various kinds of tongues, to another the interpretation of tongues.[14]*

You have been given many talents and abilities. God created you with a purpose and a plan for your life. *To one he gave five talents, to another two, to another one, to each according to his ability.[15]* You have the opportunity to use your talents to promote the kingdom of God. You have the opportunity to hear your master say, *"Well done, good and trustworthy slave; you have been trustworthy in a few things, I will put you in charge of many things; enter into the joy of your master."*[16]

You have been given the power of a priest, prophet, and king: a priest anointed with the power to bring God's grace into the lives of others; a prophet anointed with the power to speak God's truth into a world of darkness; a king anointed with the power to advance and promote your Father's kingdom here on earth.

You can commune with the Lover of your soul anytime you want in front of the Blessed Sacrament. God desperately desires to fill your inner sanctuary with his peaceful Presence. He desires to speak to you on a deep, personal, and intimate level. He wants to heal all your emotional wounds and is available through the quiet time spent in the Adoration Chapel, or before the Tabernacle.

You have been invited to the wedding banquet — a feast of the richest choice foods and finest choice wines. Your Father says, *"Look, I have prepared my dinner, my oxen and my fat calves have been slaughtered, and everything is ready; come to the wedding banquet."*[17]

You have a God who desires to make you his beloved bride. *You shall be a crown of beauty in the hand of the Lord, and a royal diadem in the hand of your God. For as a young man marries a young woman, so shall your builder marry you, and as the bridegroom rejoices over the bride, so shall your God rejoice over you.*[18]

You have a God so rich in mercy that he will forgive all your sins, regardless of what you have done in the past. *For as the heavens are high above the earth, so great is his steadfast love toward those who fear him; as far as the east is from the west, so far he removes our transgressions from us.*[19]

You have a God who loves you so much that he stripped himself of divinity and took on the form of a slave. He endured terrible suffering and pain on the cross to break Satan's hold over your soul. You have been bought for a price. You have been washed, redeemed, and sanctified by the blood of the Lamb.

You have been invited to spend the rest of eternity with God in heaven. What are you waiting for? Throw aside every weight and hindrance that clings so close. Start fighting the good fight of faith. Break the authority of anything that keeps you bound in a state of complacency, and start serving God in spirit and truth.

Time is short! Within the next hundred years, your personal life will come to a conclusion. The world as you know it will cease to exist and you will stand before the judgment throne of God. Are you ready to give an account of your life?

Jesus says, *"Enter through the narrow gate; for the gate is wide and the road is easy that leads to destruction, and there are many who take it. For the gate is narrow and the road is hard that leads to life, and there are few who find it."*[20] Are you traveling the hard and narrow road? Are you using your talents and gifts to promote the kingdom of God?

There's a vast cloud of witnesses calling you toward the finish line. They are calling you by name, cheering for you to fight the good fight of faith. Run the race in such a way as to win the prize. Athletes exercise self-control in all things; they do it to receive a perishable wreath. You have the opportunity to receive a golden crown!

Rise to your feet, all you mighty warriors of God!

The Spirit of God says, "Come!"

You are hereby commissioned!

NOTES

All the names in this book have been changed to protect the individuals' identity. The conversations recorded represent an accurate description of events, but not an actual word-for-word account.

Chapter 1 – The Vision
1. Gustave Doré, a detail of "The War Against Gibeon," *The Bible Gallery*, (New York: Cassell & Company 1880) Joshua 10.
2. Hebrews 11:33–34.
3. 2 Corinthians 11:27.
4. Luke 10:19.
5. Matthew 17:20.
6. Revelation 22:17.

Chapter 2 – The Enemy
1. Gustave Doré, a detail of "Death on a Pale Horse," *The Bible Gallery* (New York: Cassell & Company 1880) Revelation 6:8.
2. John 12:31.
3. John 18:36.
4. Luke 4:6–7.
5. John 8:44.
6. Luke 11:24–26.
7. 2 Corinthians 12:7.
8. Luke 4:39.

9. Matthew 17:18.
10. Luke 13:12.
11. Luke 13:16.
12. Mark 5:2–9.
13. Mark 5:11–13.
14. Matthew 4:3.
15. Job 2:6–7.

Chapter 3 – Worldview
1. Eyck, Jan Van, a detail of "The Last Judgment," All Rights Reserved, (The Metropolitan Museum of Art, Fletcher Fund, 1933, 33.92B), used with permission.
2. Revelation 12:7–9.
3. Revelation 12:12.
4. Genesis 3:1.
5. Genesis 3:5.
6. Genesis 4:6–7.
7. Genesis 5:24.
8. Genesis 6:6–7.
9. Genesis 1:7 Cf. Genesis 7:11.
10. Exodus 24:7.
11. Exodus 20:4.
12. Deuteronomy 18:9–12.
13. Jeremiah 2:2,5,7,12 & 13.
14. Matthew 4:3.
15. Matthew 4:4.
16. Matthew 4:6.
17. Matthew 4:7.
18. Matthew 27:30.
19. Matthew 27:46.

Chapter 4 – Open Doors
1. Gustave Doré, a detail of "The Death of Samson," *The Bible Gallery* (New York: Cassell & Company 1880) Judges 16.
2. John 8:34.
3. Galatians 5:21.
4. Genesis 2:24 Cf. 1 Corinthians 6:16.
5. Matthew 5:28.

6.   James 1:13.
7.   2 Corinthians 11:14.
8.   Catechism of the Catholic Church: 2116 - Cf. Deut 18:10;
     Jer 29:8.
9.   1 Corinthians 6:18.
10. 2 Corinthians 6:14, 15 & 17.

Chapter 5 – Taking Authority
1.   Gustave Doré, a detail of "Elijah Destroying the Messengers
     of Ahaziah," *The Bible Gallery* (New York: Cassell &
     Company 1880) 2 Kings 1.
2.   Joshua 1:2, 3, 7 & 9.
3.   Joshua 5:13.
4.   Joshua 5:14.
5.   Joshua 5:14.
6.   Joshua 6:2–5.
7.   Joshua 7:7.
8.   Joshua 7:10–12.
9.   Joshua 7:19.
10. Joshua 7:20–21.
11. Luke 10:19.
12. 2 Kings 6:15.
13. 2 Kings 6:16–17.
14. Hebrews 1:14.
15. Catechism of the Catholic Church: 336 & 329 - Cf. Mt
     18:10; Lk 16:22; Ps 34:7; 91:10-13; Job 33:23-24; Zech
     1:12; Tob 12:12. St. Basil, Adv. Eunomium III, 1: PG 29,
     656B. Mt 18:10; Ps 103:20.
16. Revelation 12:12 & 20:10.
17. 2 Corinthians 4:4.
18. Catechism of the Catholic Church: 873 & 783 - AA2. Cf.
     John Paul II, RH 18-21.

Chapter 6 – Full Armor of God
1.   Gustave Doré, a detail of "Daniel in the Lions' Den,"
     The Bible Gallery (New York: Cassell & Company 1880)
     Daniel 6.
2.   Ephesians 6:10–17.

3.   Mark 2:7.
4.   Mark 2:8–11.
5.   John 20:21–23.
6.   Catechism of the Catholic Church: 1538 - Cf. Acts 1:8; 1
       Tim 4:14; 2 Tim 1:6.
7.   John 6:53 & 56.
8.   2 Timothy 3:12.
9.   Matthew 5:10.
10.   Hebrews 12:7, 8 & 11.
11.   Galatians 5:16–17.
12.   Matthew 4:4. Cf. Deuteronomy 8:3.
13.   Catechism of the Catholic Church: 905 & 904 - St. Thomas
       Aquinas, STh. III, 71, 4ad3.
14.   John 8:31–32.
15.   Hebrews 4:12.
16.   Matthew 5:32.
17.   Matthew 17:20–21.

Chapter 7 – A Warrior's Faith
1.   Gustave Doré, a detail of "Christ Stilling the Tempest," *The
       Bible Gallery* (New York: Cassell & Company 1880)
       Matthew 8:23–27.
2.   Matthew 6:25 & 30.
3.   Matthew 8:25.
4.   Matthew 8:26.
5.   Matthew 8:27.
6.   Matthew 17:15–16.
7.   Matthew 17:17.
8.   Matthew 17:19.
9.   Matthew 17:20-21.
10.   Matthew 14:23–24.
11.   Matthew 14:26.
12.   Matthew 14:27.
13.   Matthew 14:28.
14.   Matthew 14:29.
15.   Matthew 14:29–30.
16.   Matthew 14:31–33.

Chapter 8 – A Warrior's Love

1. Gustave Doré, a detail of "Close of the Crucifixion," *The Bible Gallery* (New York: Cassell & Company 1880) Luke 23.
2. Richard Wurmbrand, *In God's Underground* (Bartlesville, OK: Living Sacrifice Book Company, 1968), pp. 228–229. www.persecution.com. Used with permission.
3. Richard Wurmbrand, *From Suffering to Triumph* (Grand Rapids, MI: Kregel Publications, 1993), pp. 49–51. www.persecution.com. Used with permission.
4. Unknown author, *The Bridge.*
5. Luke 23:34.
6. Matthew 26:39.

Chapter 9 – The Commissioning

1. Perugino, a detail of "Christ Delivering the Keys to Saint Peter," *The Vatican its History its Treasures* (New York: Letters and Arts Publishing Co. 1914) p. 74 Matthew 16: 18–19.
2. Luke 17:6 .
3. Matthew 17:20–21.
4. John 14:13-14.
5. Luke 10:18–19.
6. Catechism of the Catholic Church: 336 & 329 Cf. Mt 18:10; Lk 16:22; Ps 34:7; 91:10-13; Job 33:23–24; Zeck 1:12; Tob 12:12. St. Basil, Adv. Eunomium III, 1: PG 29, 656B Mt 18:10; Ps 103:20.
7. Matthew 16:18–19.
8. Matthew 16:18.
9. John 6:53.
10. Hebrews 4:12.
11. Catechism of the Catholic Church: p. 4. section 2.
12. Catechism of the Catholic Church: 1265 - 2 Cor 5:17; 2 Pet 1:4; cf. Gal 4:5-7. Cf. 1 Cor 6:15; 12:27; Rom 8:17. Cf. 1 Cor 6:19.
13. Catechism of the Catholic Church: 1303 - Cf. LG 11. Cf. Council of Florence (1439); DS 1319; LG 11; 12.

14.   1 Corinthians 12:8–10.
15.   Matthew 25:15.
16.   Matthew 25:21.
17.   Matthew 22:4.
18.   Isaiah 62:3 & 5.
19.   Psalm 103:11–12.
20.   Matthew 7:13–14.

ABOUT THE AUTHOR

Robert Abel's purpose and passion in life is speaking God's truth unto today's generation.

He lives in Denver, Colorado where he leads a homeless ministry, and helps others heal through counseling sessions and healing seminars.

If you would like Robert to speak at your parish, please contact him at:

www.CatholicWarriors.com

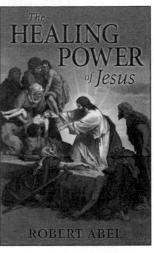

Healing Power for the Heart
by Robert Abel

Do you feel distant from God's love? Are you searching for ultimate fulfillment in life?

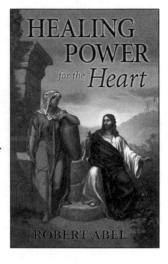

Jesus came so that you may have life and have it more *abundantly!* He wants to heal all your wounds and fill your heart with his incredible love.

In this book, Robert Abel will show you how to establish a deeper and more passionate relationship with Jesus. The spiritual exercises on these life-giving pages have the power to break all forms of bondage in your life, and bring the Lord's healing power into all your traumatic past experiences.

Jesus wants to take you on an exciting adventure deep within the recesses of your soul. He is calling you right now, *"Come to me, all you that are weary and are carrying heavy burdens, and I will give you rest."*

What are you waiting for? Embark upon the adventure of a lifetime. Open your heart and experience the fullness of God's extravagant love.

Available at your local bookstore or online at
www.HealingPowerMinistries.com

72 Pages — $5.99 U.S.

If you would like to participate in our ministry, please consider spreading the message from *The Catholic Warrior*. To purchase additional copies of this book for ministry purposes, or to make a donation, please use the following information:

Number of Copies	Ministry Price
3	$25
6	$40
9	$50

These prices include tax and free shipping within the United States. For shipments to other countries, please contact us. Thank you for your generous donations.

Mail your payment to:

Valentine Publishing House
The Catholic Warrior
P.O. Box 27422
Denver, Colorado 80227